REMEMBERING
ANITA COBBY

THE CASE, THE HUSBAND, THE AFTERMATH – 30 YEARS ON

MARK MORRI

EBURY
PRESS

An Ebury Press book
Published by Random House Australia Pty Ltd
Level 3, 100 Pacific Highway, North Sydney NSW 2060
www.randomhouse.com.au

Penguin
Random House
Australia

First published by Ebury Press in 2016

Random House Books is part of the Penguin Random House group of companies whose addresses can be found at global.penguinrandomhouse.com/offices.

National Library of Australia
Cataloguing-in-Publication Entry

Morri, Mark, author
Remembering Anita Cobby: the case, the husband, the aftermath – 30 years on/Mark Morri

ISBN 978 1 92532 415 0 (paperback)

Cobby, Anita
Cobby, John
Murder – New South Wales – Sydney
Nurses – New South Wales – Sydney – Biography

364.1523099441

Cover design by Luke Causby/Blue Cork
Internal design and typesetting by Post Pre-Press, Australia
Printed in Australia by Griffin Press, an accredited ISO AS/NZS 14001:2004 Environmental Management System printer

Random House Australia uses papers that are natural, renewable and recyclable products and made from wood grown in sustainable forests. The logging and manufacturing processes are expected to conform to the environmental regulations of the country of origin.

CONTENTS

To my wife, Nicole Payten-Morri, my son Mitchell Morri and his brother Thomas Coleman, a beautiful young man lost to this world far too early

AUTHOR'S NOTE

Remembering Anita Cobby is more than recounting the murder of a beautiful young woman and the many lives it touched. It is a story about John Cobby – her long forgotten husband who, after a lifetime of grief and irrational guilt, is finally finding himself.

There is no way to soften the hideous crime against Anita or how murder can take the soul of the living as well as the dead, but at the same time I hope this book conveys the notion that love and support can help those living victims.

The detectives still affected by working on the investigation thirty years ago helped enormously in providing their insight and details about the case. My thanks goes especially to former Detectives Ian Kennedy and Graham Rosetta, who let me into their homes and spent hours checking details over and over again against their memories and notes. Lawyers Leigh Johnson and Simon Joyner were equally generous with their time.

I am particularly indebted to the NSW Police Force and the head of the NSW Homicide Squad, Detective Superintendent Michael Willing, for allowing me access to Anita's file, which was invaluable in helping to record the events surrounding Anita's death as accurately as possible.

Some paperwork is missing after thirty years and memories have faded but, where possible, every fact presented has been checked and rechecked. John was insistent that I try to verify all his recollections with anyone I could or against police records. At times, his memory, those of the police and others seemed slightly at odds with official records and other people's recollections.

The only glaring fact misreported over the years – and again recently – is that John was driving to the south coast to see friends when he heard the news on the radio that Anita's body had been found. His sister and police records all verify John's account of heading *north*, believing Anita may be on the NSW Central Coast.

I also want to thank my wife, Nicole, and my brother, Rodney, who gave me incredible moral support throughout the writing of the book. Likewise, the input of John's sister Gaynor and his son Daniel were crucial in putting many things in context.

Remembering Anita Cobby would not have been possible but for the bravery of John finally telling his story. As a person who has become a good friend, I wish him all the best.

PROLOGUE

Tuesday 4 February 1986

IT WAS A BEAUTIFUL AFTERNOON. Male nurse John Cobby was feeling pretty good, even if he was slightly anxious that his wife hadn't turned up for work at Sydney Hospital the day before. He and Anita were coming out of a rough patch in their marriage, during which they had been temporarily living apart. But the sun was shining as he drove his beloved 1983 green Escort panel van up the Pacific Highway to the Central Coast, with the radio going full blast on 2SM. It was the number one pop music station of the day. He and Anita loved to listen and sing along whenever they were driving – especially on their frequent trips to the snow. He started thinking back to those weekends, when they'd listen over and over to Madonna or Cold Chisel. It gave his spirits a lift and a smile crept across his face.

His sister, Gaynor, had rented a holiday house near the water at Shelly Beach to celebrate her birthday, and that was where he was heading. He planned to go for a surf as soon as he arrived, to cool off after the drive.

He was looking forward to seeing Anita. He was telling himself she would be safe and well with Gaynor; they were great friends. Even though John and Anita were having a break from their relationship, the two women had been seeing a lot of each other. Their friendship didn't seem to have been affected by the strange restlessness that had overtaken Anita since she and John had returned from overseas in the middle of the previous year.

In John's eyes, Anita was as beautiful as ever, as full of love for life and the people around her as she had always been. Those things would never change in her, of that he was sure.

Since they had decided to take time out six weeks ago, the tension between the two of them had gradually eased. Now they were in constant contact.

His thoughts turned to the previous weekend at his nan's place, when he and Anita had spent hours talking things out and their problems had started to seem less important. They'd ended up pouring their hearts out to each other and realised that they were too much in love to end their relationship. Afterwards they'd made love.

In the days following, that feeling of closeness had remained. Things between them felt much more settled. Now they were making plans to find a house to rent and restart their lives as a couple. During the past week they had also spoken about spending time on the Central Coast with Gaynor.

So with everything looking up, why was he feeling on edge? There was nothing to worry about, he assured himself. Even though Anita had missed work yesterday, he was sure she was fine; she was probably sitting in the sun with Gaynor right now. The surf would soon clear his head, sort out his strange mood.

Then the news came on the radio and the words leaped out at him: 'The naked body of a young woman has been found in a paddock at Prospect in western Sydney. Police are yet to identify her.'

It was as though a brick had hit John Cobby in the face. Straightaway he had a horrible feeling that the announcer was talking about Anita. The thing that had been gnawing away at him, setting his nerves on edge all day, he now realised, was that she would never have skipped work, never have failed to let someone else know she couldn't make it.

He swerved to the side of the highway and found an emergency phone, there for stranded motorists to use. His hands shaking, he got on the line and screamed at the operator, demanding and begging in the same breath to be put through to Anita's parents' home. He wasn't making any sense, but eventually they put him through.

A woman came on the line; it could have been either Anita's sister, Kathryn, or her mother, Grace, better known as Peg. All John registered were the words, 'You've got to get back here, John', then the click as the line went dead.

Looking around, John realised he was near Peats Ridge, about 80 kilometres north of Sydney. Heart pounding, he raced back to the car and made a U-turn – crossing all four lanes and mounting the median strip – then sped towards Blacktown.

The drive was a blur. Functioning like some kind of robot, he changed gears, negotiated the traffic and even ran several red lights without incident. All the while a loop of thoughts was running through his head: *This can't be happening. It can't be her. We're going to be together for the rest of our lives.*

Finally he pulled into the driveway of the Lynches' home in O'Sullivan Street and made his way to the back of the house.

Before he knocked on the door, he dropped to the steps, put his head in his hands and wept.

*

3

The night before, Peg Lynch had called John's mother, Terri Cobby, asking if Anita was with John. Terri had said she wasn't sure, but she had known exactly how to reach John and tell him to ring his mother-in-law. Immediately, she had rung The Prophet restaurant in Surry Hills, where he was having dinner with his father, Noel, and an old friend named Sue.

Michael, the restaurant owner, came over and told John his mum was on the phone. Minutes later, he was talking to Mrs Lynch and telling her everything he knew. He and Anita were in daily contact and John had spoken to her the previous morning – Sunday – hoping to arrange a catch-up after she'd finished work. Anita had put him off. She explained that she had made arrangements to go out with friends for a meal that evening, and she'd already told her mum and dad that after dinner she would be heading straight back to the family home, where she had been staying during the separation. John knew that Anita wouldn't have wanted to let her parents down.

As soon as John hung up after talking to his mother-in-law he prepared to go, leaving his meal unfinished, so he could head over to the Lynch home. His father was disappointed he was going so soon; they'd barely been at the restaurant an hour. But he understood when John quickly explained that Anita had not turned up to work that day as expected, and that John was worried. She had never done anything like that before. Anita was no party girl and was usually completely reliable. The Lynches had been anxiously ringing some of her friends who might know something, and he wanted to help with the search.

John dropped off Sue at Lilli Pilli in Sydney's southern suburbs before heading west to Blacktown, stopping at a bottle shop on the way to buy scotch.

When he arrived at the Lynches' three-bedroom weatherboard home, Anita's father, Garry, was in the living room. An

4

agitated Peg kept coming in and out, attempting to keep herself busy and trying not to worry about Anita.

Skipping the niceties, John asked Garry to fill him in on the situation, then quizzed him insistently about what he'd done to find Anita. He'd reported her disappearance to the police hours earlier, but had he rung all the hospitals in Sydney? What friends had he called?

Not surprisingly, this interrogation got Garry's back up. In the past the two men had always managed to skate over their mutual dislike. This time, it was not so easy.

For the next hour or so the pair sat there drinking scotch and ringing around but getting nowhere. Frustrated by the lack of progress, they became steadily angrier with each other. Eventually, drunk and fearing he was about to explode at his father-in-law, John got back into his car and returned to his mother's place in Rockdale. When he and Anita had split, his mother had put him up in a caravan out the front of her house. It was a temporary move, as John was sure he would get back together with Anita and hadn't even thought about renting or moving somewhere by himself.

John went to sleep, having decided to take the day off and drive up to the Central Coast the next morning. The plan of action eased the knot in his stomach a little.

The next day, waking up late with a hangover, but by now fairly certain that Anita was with Gaynor, he set out on the drive north. There were no mobile phones back then and all John had was the address Gaynor had given him for the house she had rented at Shelly Beach.

As he drove, his conviction that Anita was safe and with Gaynor grew. It stood to reason: a week ago all three of them had spent the weekend together at Rockdale, and it had been fantastic. Anita must have made a snap decision to take the previous day off and spend more time with his sister.

The drive was soothing. Every minute behind the wheel

was bringing John closer to being with Anita. Soon he would be telling Gaynor they were getting back together – that was, if Anita hadn't already told her. It was highly likely she had, given how close the two women were.

Then came that radio bulletin, destroying his daydreams in seconds.

No one had actually said in so many words that Anita was dead, but John had an overwhelming sense of foreboding. There had been a peculiar urgency in the voice on the other end of the phone at Anita's parents' place.

But as he pushed himself up from the steps, and braced himself to go through the door and hear someone spell out the horror for him, there was another nightmare he had to face.

John Cobby, estranged husband of nurse Anita Cobby, was the prime suspect in her murder.

CHAPTER 1

'Did you do it?'

Evening, Tuesday 4 February 1986

JOHN COBBY SAT IN A SMALL INTERVIEW ROOM in Blacktown police station, a totally broken man. A few hours before, he had been told that his wife, Anita, had been brutally murdered and her bloodied body found in a paddock. At this stage, that was pretty much all he knew. Police had yet to tell him of the horrendous injuries she had suffered as she fought for her life.

Police had deduced that the badly beaten body found in Prospect was almost certainly that of missing woman Anita Cobby. As the autopsy got under way, two detectives – Detective Sergeant Ian Kennedy and Senior Constable Garry Heskett – had gone straight around to the Lynch home to break the grim news and broach the topic of formal identification.

It is a duty that police are carefully trained to perform. Despite the carefully thought out procedures and protocols and the matter-of-factness afforded by the simple, formal language, it is never an easy job. This time, it was going to be extremely tough.

The only piece of jewellery or clothing left on Anita was a ring made up of three interlocking bands of white gold – a Russian wedding ring. As soon as Detective Ian Kennedy showed it to Grace, Garry and Kathryn, they confirmed that it was hers. The devastation they must have felt at that point can hardly be imagined.

When Kathryn commented that it looked a bit rusty, the officers had to explain that she was mistaken. What she thought was rust was in fact her sister's blood.

After John Cobby arrived at the house, he also immediately recognised the ring. He had put it on Anita's finger himself, when they were married on 27 March 1982.

Detective Kennedy led a stunned John Cobby to the back steps of the Lynch house – out of earshot of everyone else – and asked him if he was prepared to accompany the detectives to the morgue and formally identify Anita's body.

The homicide detective knew how harrowing that step was going to be. Seeing the body of a loved one, dead through misadventure, is a huge ordeal. And Anita had suffered horrific injuries, so in this case the viewing was going to be traumatising. The detectives were hoping to be able to spare the parents that agonising experience. They were also anxious to speak to John alone, observe his reactions, and get a feeling for how things were between him and his wife.

But they were to be disappointed: John Cobby shook his head vehemently. He was unable to face the ordeal of viewing the body; then it would be far too real.

Grace Lynch had already volunteered to go to the morgue: she explained to the officers that she was a nurse and had seen plenty of dead bodies before. But they wouldn't have a bar of it. They didn't want to put a woman, a mother, through this.

There was no alternative. If John Cobby wasn't up to it, the burden would have to fall on Garry Lynch. Ray Eedens, Garry's other son-in-law, agreed to go too – not to identify the body but to support Garry. This was at the suggestion of police.

Kennedy and Heskett drove Garry and Ray to the morgue at Westmead Hospital. The instant the covering was carefully pulled back to reveal a glimpse of the face, Garry Lynch's knees buckled. The two lawmen had to hold him upright. Garry managed to get out the words: 'I wish I could say it's someone else's daughter, but it's not, is it?'

The detectives gave Garry time to compose himself then all four made their way sombrely back to the car. During the return trip to Blacktown, Kennedy and Heskett talked Garry through a little of what lay ahead for the distressed family. There was going to be a police investigation and there would be a lot of media attention.

The identification was just one step in a long list of police procedures, many of them painful for the loved ones. As is standard practice in a homicide, everyone in the victim's immediate circle would have to be questioned. The police started with John Cobby.

Later, he would recall that darkness was falling when he entered the police station. As to what happened immediately afterwards, he would only remember brief snatches, all of them painful.

The conversation was gentle at first. But soon the questions started coming thick and fast. Where was he at the time of the murder? How were things between the two of them? Over and over again. Then they escalated into accusations:

'Did you kill her, John? You know you did.'

'Did you pay for someone to do it?'

The officers firing the questions at him were the two who had visited the Lynch home. One, a huge man, was doing most of the interrogating and making most of the accusations. The other went in and out of the room and seemed softer. It was the classic good-cop-bad-cop scenario. But this was no TV show. Everything was alarmingly real.

For Cobby, the onslaught was relentless, nightmarish. He found himself off balance in every way possible. His mind seemed to go into a weird state, to disconnect from what was happening. In a moment of reconnection, he realised he was backed up against a wall. His head was spinning and he thought he might be sick. Then he was crumbling to the ground, putting his hand in the air and saying, 'Yep, I did it. Must have.'

Anita was dead; that was all he knew. Nothing made sense. Nothing mattered.

Why an innocent man would profess to have killed his wife is a complete mystery. Was it stress? Shock? Guilt at not having protected her? An extreme reaction to the discomfort of being interrogated?

Who could say why, but his mind raced into places he couldn't understand. It was like being in a horror movie. He felt he deserved to be taken out and shot in the head. At least that would put an end to the pain, the ghastly reality.

The big detective doing the majority of the questioning, Ian 'Speed' Kennedy, was a former first-grade rugby union player with Randwick. He had earned his reputation at Coogee Oval as a rugged, menacing second-row forward.

Coincidentally, John had grown up in the same area and played junior football for Randwick Colts. But he had never crossed paths with Speed Kennedy; by then Kennedy was already a well-respected homicide detective.

Cobby's abiding memory of that interview is of how big Kennedy seemed: a copper twice his own size, firing questions at him. That, and the fact that Anita was gone. Every question reinforced it, while his mind kept fighting it, thinking, *This isn't happening.* Basically, John Cobby was a mess.

To say the interview didn't go well is an understatement.

In the eyes of the investigators, John hadn't helped himself when he didn't want to identify Anita. Given the historic link between homicides and what's now referred to as 'intimate partner violence', Cobby was probably correct in his assumption that the cops believed that he had committed the crime and that he couldn't face what he had done. Another factor was that Garry Lynch wasn't overly fond of him, and Cobby might well have said a few uncomplimentary things about his father-in-law. Equally, his father-in-law might have had a bit to say about him.

Twelve days after the police interview, Speed Kennedy made an entry in the investigators' bible – the running sheet. In a major criminal investigation, every scrap of information – from phone calls to interviews to police statements – is logged in a running sheet, along with observations by the detectives assigned to the case. These notes are constantly reviewed, for instance to keep an eye out for leads that might not have been followed up properly, to cross-check all the details in order to spot whether a witness might have been lying, or to correct the timeline leading up to the death as new information comes in.

Kennedy's entry reads as follows:

At 6.15 pm this date attended premises at Tramway St Mascot re information re running sheet.

There spoke to Gaynor Cobby, sister of John Cobby, husband of the deceased. She stated her boyfriend Michael Davies resides at the premises, she frequently stays there herself. The deceased Anita Cobby stayed overnight there the week before her death. She did confirm that she was staying at Shelly Beach the weekend of the murder, which is in accord with John Cobby's statement that he was travelling to Central Coast on 4.2.86 to locate his sister and hopefully his missing wife, when he heard of the discovery of a female's body at Blacktown on the car radio.

Police had now carefully checked out every detail of John Cobby's statement – and found no discrepancies. 'It would appear the deceased was murdered late Sunday evening or early Monday morning (February 2 or the morning of February 3). Her husband's alibi has been verified by Sue XX,' Detective Kennedy's notes recorded.

A few days after the interview with John, police received a phone call that further backed up John's version of events. Restaurateur Michael Souri told police that John was in his restaurant when Mrs Cobby rang and told him Anita had not turned up to work on the Monday:

> He informed police that about 8 pm on the 3.2.86 he was at his family restaurant The Prophet, 274 Cleveland Street, Surry Hills, when he answered the telephone and a woman he knows as Terri Cobby rang looking for her son, John Cobby. He ascertained that John's wife, Anita Cobby, had been missing. After the telephone call John Cobby left the premises. It was further ascertained that John Cobby arrived at the restaurant about 7 pm with his father and a friend of John's. Souri stated that he hasn't seen the missing Anita Cobby for a period of a month but knew that John and her had separated.

In other words, within days of that scarring interrogation, police had crossed John Cobby off the list of suspects. Despite his sudden confession, some of the officers on the case never thought for a minute that Cobby could have committed the crime, believing from the word go that it was an act of random violence committed by several people.

But while the investigation moved on, John Cobby remained a shattered man.

Thirty years would pass before he could examine, let alone come to terms with, certain aspects of what happened to

Anita – and to him, not that he likes to put the two together in one sentence. Scratch just below the surface of this quiet man and there are raw emotions from that interview with Detective Kennedy. Put simply, since 4 February 1986, Cobby's life has been blighted.

Yet he holds no grudge against those officers who questioned him that night, Speed Kennedy included. 'He had a job to do. I know now I was the prime suspect and they had to ask me, but at the time my mind wasn't working that way.'

A couple of small comments about John Cobby made by Anita's friends sowed seeds of doubt about him in the minds of investigators. Like Anita, Lyn Bradshaw and Elaine Bray were nurses at Sydney Hospital. Lyn, Elaine and Anita were close. Recently they had been working the same shift, and they had all had dinner together after work on the Sunday, which was later established as the evening of the murder. According to the running notes, 'Both women stated that the deceased left her husband late in 1985 and moved in with her parents at Sullivan Street, Blacktown. They have stated that her husband rang several times a week at work in an attempt to get her back. Apparently he was devastated by the separation.'

There was something else in the statements made by Bradshaw and Bray that had drawn the detectives' attention: Anita had mentioned she had recently been seeing a fair bit of a fellow nurse at Sydney Hospital, a man named Ian McIntosh. Police noted that Ian McIntosh and John Cobby had known each other for years, whereas Anita and Ian had got to know each other relatively recently.

That explained why John Cobby had rocketed up the suspect list in those early hours and days of the investigation.

Police were dealing with a recently separated husband who was constantly ringing up, attempting to get back with his estranged wife – plus her friends had described him as devastated and desperate for a reconciliation. Had he found out that his friend Ian was seeing Anita behind his back and killed her in a fit of jealous rage? There were signs that strongly suggested the murder was a crime of hate and possibly unpremeditated passion.

Later it was determined that the relationship between Ian and Anita was purely platonic. But for the time being, the situation aroused suspicion.

It was no wonder that the media were immediately fascinated by the murder of this stunning young woman. Anita Cobby was a former beauty queen, and a kind-hearted nurse for whom no one had a harsh word. Hers was the worst murder Sydney had ever seen. Right from the start it was an emotionally charged investigation that had journalists desperate for information – and I was one of them.

The Anita Cobby case was the first major story of my crime-reporting career. I was twenty-five years old and had only been on the crime beat for a year, on the now-defunct *Daily Mirror*. I still hadn't earned my stripes and was very much a junior crime reporter. At the start, I had no idea that the murder would capture the attention of Sydney so strongly. Or that decades later I would become immersed in the lives of John and his late wife.

Statistically, murders tend to be committed by someone close to the victim – often a friend or family member, particularly if they are a spouse or lover. In this case, John and Anita had just split. John Cobby was a person of interest, to put it mildly, and I became part of the media pack pursuing him.

Like the police, the media had no real idea of who was responsible. A new boyfriend perhaps? Or was it just a random killing? Everyone had a theory, and in those early days we spent hours in the pub discussing who might have done it. The cops were being tight-lipped about the husband both publicly and in private, raising the media's suspicions that they were looking at him as a suspect. From the instant the body was found, every single day the press was dominated by a headline about the murder, and this went on for a good six weeks. Interviews with neighbours were aired repeatedly. Daily updates were being given by Ian Kennedy. Garry Lynch was continually going on radio and talking to newspaper reporters, begging them to help catch his daughter's killer or killers.

Yet the media would find John Cobby extremely elusive.

Before he left the Blacktown police station that first day, there was one thing John very much wanted, and that was Anita's ring. He had bought it for her for their wedding, and Anita had loved it.

At some stage, one of the detectives came into the room and put down a small plastic exhibit bag with the ring in it. The records show that police handed the ring over to John and he signed for it on the night his wife's body was found.

'We had no reason to keep it and he wanted it. I don't think I had even signed it into evidence,' Speed Kennedy told me many years later.

John remembers it was handed to him, or perhaps put down on the table in front of him. He opened it, this small plastic bag, which looked kind of yellow, and there was the ring. To his shock and disbelief, it had Anita's blood all over it. He can still picture it: yet another image seared into his memory.

He grabbed the ring in a stupor and they let him leave the station.

Driving back home, he held that ring tightly as he thought of Anita. It was all he had of her now.

CHAPTER 2

The years before

1980

JOHN COBBY FIRST LAID EYES ON raven-haired Anita Lynch at Sydney Hospital, where she was following in the footsteps of her mother, Peg, by training to be a nurse. She was twenty years old, and stunning.

'Just these ringlets of hair everywhere. God, she was beautiful and, I thought, far too good for me. I saw her in the corridors of the nurses' quarters where we lived. She was what was called a PTS nurse back then. A provisional trainee student.'

Anita was six weeks into her training and John, aged twenty-three, was in his third year. He had had a break from it a couple of years earlier and now was starting his career again at Sydney Hospital.

When he met Anita he was instantly smitten, but held back. 'I was thinking to myself, *She will never go out with me.*'

Well over thirty years later, he can still picture her smile that day. It dazzled him. Sadly, it would become a memory that still tortures him most days, reminding him of a love not lost, but ripped from him.

As a kid, John had been a bit on the wild side. He spent a few years running around the working-class suburb of Redfern. When he was about eight, his family moved to the seaside suburb of Malabar, a stone's throw from the infamous Long Bay jail, known to many Sydneysiders as the Malabar Hilton.

Becoming a nurse was never on John's radar during his schooldays at Waverley College, a Catholic boys' school in Sydney's eastern suburbs. Neither was academic life. The nearby beaches and the waves held a lot more attraction for him than study. A mischievous teenager, John learned how to use penny bungers with a cigarette filter as a delayed timer, and would regularly set off a small explosion in the school toilets. After partially blowing them up on more than one occasion, John picked up the nickname 'Bomber'.

'It would make a huge noise in the empty toilet blocks, but by the time it went off I would be sitting in the back of the classroom. Got away with it for about a year before getting caught and copped a hiding off one of the brothers.'

Despite his antics, John finished school in 1975 with a reasonable mark in the Higher School Certificate. He didn't have a clue what he wanted to do next and was happy to drift for a while. He spent the first year after school travelling around Australia with a girlfriend called Lisa before settling in Darwin for a few months.

'It wasn't long after Cyclone Tracy. I worked in a betting shop out of the Don Hotel and was making good money from it.'

The income allowed John to indulge in his great passion, surfing. He also made the occasional trip to Indonesia, when he could afford it.

On his return to Sydney, he worked night shifts as a barman at the Newtown RSL Club and would hit the beach during the day. The clientele at the club was a mixed crowd of football players, boxers and some of the city's seedier characters, including Branko Balic, a boxer who later became an enforcer for Sydney gangster Lennie McPherson. He also got to know drug dealers Paul Hayward and Warren Fellows. Hayward was a talented sportsman who played first-grade rugby league for the Newtown Jets. He was the brother-in-law of infamous Sydney gangster Neddy Smith, whom John, coincidentally, would later get to know. Haywood and Fellows were eventually implicated in the importation of huge amounts of hashish and were caught and jailed in Thailand.

'I had no idea what those guys were into. I was a young guy not long out of school and just getting enough money to survive and surf. Drugs were never ever my thing – not even dope, which was everywhere in those days.'

His father Noel had certainly mixed with some dodgy people. Noel had spent years as an SP (fixed odds) bookie, working for one of the country's most famous underworld figures, George Freeman. In those days, Freeman basically ruled Sydney.

John has no idea how well his father knew Freeman, or any of the other individuals in Freeman's orbit. The relationship between father and son became strained during John's teenage years and remained so until Noel died in 1995. He was a pretty tough sort of person and quite hard on John. It probably didn't help that Noel and Terri's marriage didn't last. The two parted early in 1980. John was always close to his mother's family

Meanwhile, John's own association with some of Sydney's more colourful characters was fleeting; he was never involved in their activities in any way.

In John's late teens, the Cobby family moved to the Central Coast, where his father was trying to set himself up as legitimate rails bookmaker at Gosford Race Club. John also developed a keen eye for horses and the odd punt. It was in his blood on his mother's side. She came from a family that had been involved in horse racing for over a century. His maternal grandmother had been very hands-on with horses, and John seemed to inherit his affinity for the animals from her. John grew up around horses and always felt very at home.

Although on the surface it appeared to be 'like father, like son', John's feelings about horse racing were totally different from his dad's. Noel was a punter and only saw horses as animals to bet on. From an early age, John loved the beauty of horses and the way they run with so much power, finding it a majestic thing to watch.

When the family first moved to the Central Coast, John was an out-of-work 19-year-old. A string of temporary jobs followed, including working at the Florida Hotel at Terrigal, then one of the Central Coast's most popular pubs. It was full of young unemployed people drinking their dole money, and tradies drinking after work. It suited John. Like most recent school-leavers, he was finding his way in life, caring little about tomorrow but living for the day and the surf conditions.

Eventually John went on the dole, but he had always earned a living and wasn't comfortable with getting a handout. He was required to attend regular interviews to prove he was making attempts to find work. After just three weeks of receiving social security, he ended up with a job at Gosford Hospital, in the laundry department.

'It was horrible work. Loading washing machines with the sheets straight off the beds. They had urine, blood and other nasty things on them.' He wanted something a little bit more interesting, so he went to the hospital administration and asked if there were any positions for wardsmen. 'Anything to get out of the laundry.'

The manager looked at John and said, 'No offence, but it involves a lot of lifting, and wardsmen are normally bigger than you. But you have a pretty good HSC, which would qualify you to start as a trainee nurse. There's a vacancy in about three months.' And that was how John Cobby ended up pursuing a career in nursing.

At first he had little to no interest in being a nurse, but he filled out the forms anyway. Two days later at 7 am, Terri Cobby knocked on the door of her son's room and told him that someone from the hospital was on the phone. A student had dropped out of the course and they wanted to interview him right then over the phone. By the end of the conversation they had made it clear that they wanted him to turn up at the hospital that morning. He knew the surf was flat and thought, *Why not go along?*

Pretty soon he was working as a first-year trainee nurse at Gosford Hospital. To the surprise of everyone concerned – himself included – he loved it. For the first time since leaving school, he had a purpose.

But his restless nature soon got the better of him – as well as an argument with a superior – and saw him head back outdoors to follow his love of surfing.

Before long, he decided to go to the snowfields and become a skiing instructor, even though he had never skied in his life. Although this dream never quite got off the ground, he ended up working in a bar in Thredbo and having a brilliant social life.

When the season ended and the work and the money ran out, once again John was back looking for work. He moved in with his grandmother at Rockdale in southern Sydney; he did this on and off in his early twenties. After two years of this itinerant lifestyle, John decided to restart his nursing career and applied to Concord Burns Hospital. They had a spot for him but said he would have to start all over again as a first-year trainee. So he applied for a position at Sydney Hospital. When they agreed to take him on as a third year, he jumped at the opportunity. It was the move that would bring him and Anita together two years later.

He moved into the nurses' quarters in Winstone Lodge, a converted motel at the bottom of Plunkett Street. He was one of thirteen male nurses – the majority of them gay – among scores of young women.

This was a golden time. The gay guys were great fun to work with and a lot of them were really good nurses. And being one of the few straight guys around in a predominantly female workforce guaranteed an abundance of female attention. He could work night shifts and surf during the day, and had somewhere to live right in the middle of the city.

There were quite a few one-night stands along the way, but every time John sincerely hoped that the girl he was with was 'the one'. Someone he could love and be with forever.

He had been seeing a lot of a girl called Leonie, a fellow nurse with whom he had much in common. John had enormous feelings for Leonie and would never have done anything intentionally to hurt her, but when Anita Lorraine Lynch walked down the hall in her nurse's uniform, everything changed.

John's feelings were beyond his control. The first time John set eyes on her, he was gobsmacked. With not a scrap of make-up on, she had the most perfect face he had ever seen. Even among the dozens of other nurses, many of them young and attractive, Anita Lynch stood out. Over and over again he told himself how beautiful she was.

But there was also a special quality about Anita, something that made her more than a pretty face. With her caring soul, she was a natural nurse, someone who sincerely felt for her patients. People warmed to her and took her into their hearts.

Initially John didn't approach Anita. He would simply give her a glance as he passed her in the hall, or maybe a nod as they walked past each other on the way to their shifts. In those days, he was a fairly confident young man with blue eyes and the blond locks of a surfer. Still, he was intimidated by her looks and assumed he had no hope of dating such an attractive woman. He asked around and found out she had won the Miss

Western Suburbs beauty pageant, and the gorgeous girl with the tumbling hair seemed even more out of reach.

Here he was, a kid from Redfern, 5 foot 10 (1.78 m), and 10 stone (63.5 kg) wringing wet. She was a former beauty queen who had been photographed with Neville Wran, the Premier of New South Wales.

Convinced Anita was out of his league, John tried to put her out of his head. But every couple of days he would catch a glimpse of her luxuriant hair and his head would again fill with fantasies of them together.

But things seemed to get better when he found himself talking to her one day in the corridor of the nurses' quarters, where she was also living. Was it his imagination, or did she go out of her way to prolong the conversation? He was thinking, *She's just being polite. She couldn't be interested in me.*

But she was, and he was over the moon, as infatuated as a schoolboy. Somehow he plucked up the nerve to ask her out, and a few days later the pair were sitting opposite each other at The Prophet restaurant in Surry Hills. They talked for hours, drank some wine and kept talking. There was an instant connection.

On the surface, they appeared to come from different worlds, both socially and geographically. Anita had grown up in Blacktown, the heartland of Sydney's western suburbs. Hers was a typical suburban lifestyle, with two loving parents and a little sister. Anita had come through the public school system, attending Evans High in Blacktown, where she had been a model student.

John, on the other hand, had been educated at a private school in Sydney's eastern suburbs, and was slightly anti-authoritarian. He'd had little interest in school, though he always used to do enough work to get by and achieve reasonable grades. His family was close-knit, but he had a fractured relationship with his father.

In temperament they were different as well. Anita, far more straitlaced and studious than John, was shy about her stunning good looks. By contrast, John was a worldly character, having been exposed to the rough and tumble of city life from his early years. A natural story-teller, he had an abundance of yarns about punters winning massive amounts of money at the racetrack and the characters he had met trackside or while working as a barman in Sydney's inner suburbs.

The night after their first magical date, they did it all over again. The same thing, same restaurant. John wanted to marry Anita from very early on.

Something else had happened on Anita and John's first outing: the beginning of their longstanding friendship with the owner of The Prophet restaurant, Michael Souri.

'That first date, I remember them being totally into each other,' says Souri. 'She was beautiful, with this dazzling smile. In all the time I knew her, I never saw her in a bad mood. Always smiling. The two of them were so happy whenever I saw them together.'

Over the following years, John and Anita were to become regulars at The Prophet. It was as though they owned the place. They would pop into the kitchen to see what was being cooked and to say hello to the staff. The Prophet was one of Sydney's busiest Lebanese restaurants then. It was especially popular with Sydney's racing crowd.

Not only was John a charming larrikin – perfectly at ease in the flashy world of punters, racehorse owners and jockeys – but he was also a healing presence for the sick and less fortunate lying in hospital. It was an irresistible mix, and Anita fell for it. Equally, the appeal of the beauty from the west who loved drawing, the outdoors and laughter was intoxicating for John.

Things moved quickly for the two lovebirds. Those early dinners were swiftly followed up with a weekend away in the snow. From then on they were a couple and pretty much living together in each other's rooms.

Around Sydney Hospital the word was out. John the player and Anita the beauty queen were an item.

March 1982

It was just over a year after their first romantic dinner when the pair decided to get married.

'There was no bended-knee proposal or anything that dramatic,' John recalls. 'It was almost unspoken and taken for granted we would get married.

'We told people we were getting married, and the next thing you know, everyone just took over.'

Anita and her mother joined forces with Gaynor and Terri Cobby to plan the wedding in earnest. John was swept along in the whirlwind, happy to let the women around him make all the decisions. They had far more interest in the details of wedding planning than he did. He suspected that any suggestions he might make would probably be passed over anyway, and he was fine with that.

Anita was glowing and the happiest he had ever seen her. The date for the wedding was set for late March 1982.

One evening, when John came home from work he found Anita in a state of excitement. Somehow he doubted that it had anything to do with wedding arrangements. The smile on her face told him she had a secret she was bursting to share. He waited, knowing it would come out soon, letting her savour the moment. Before long, she snuggled into him and told him she was pregnant.

Like everything else to do with their relationship, the prospect of a baby seemed to be a natural progression of their life together.

'We were happy. Anita was ecstatic, and while we kept the news low-key, we didn't keep it a secret.'

According to Gaynor, the couple let only a few members of their family in on their news. She describes the pregnancy as an added bonus for a couple very much in love.

A few weeks before the wedding, John found Anita crying in the bedroom. He held her tight as she broke the news: she had lost the baby. 'It was about nine weeks into the pregnancy, and it hurt us like hell, especially Anita. She was pretty upset . . . It might sound strange but although we were sad, we weren't devastated. We were both nurses and knew these things often happen and usually for a reason. Maybe something hadn't been right with the baby.'

Above all, John and Anita had no sense of rush. They would be spending a lifetime together. There would be plenty of time to have kids.

The wedding went ahead without a hitch. The marriage ceremony was performed by the Cobby family's local priest, Father Frank, at Rockdale Catholic Church. John's mother and grandmother did the catering for the small reception at the Cobby family home. 'We didn't want anything fancy. It was a typical Australian wedding, with nothing pretentious about it. Just two young people in love.'

John's father wasn't among the guests and well-wishers that day; he hadn't been invited. John's parents had split a couple years earlier, and his father had been in and out of John's life ever since. He had never been a permanent fixture, really, although he remained close to Gaynor.

'He and I were pretty much estranged at that point. Dad was a pretty hard kind of guy. I didn't have much to do with him for years, although after Anita's death he was around a bit at first – probably out of some sort of guilt.'

Gaynor remembers 27 March 1982 perfectly. 'It was a lovely, simple occasion, and Anita loved it. She glowed. She and John just smiled all night. Anita looked simply gorgeous in a lovely broderie anglaise dress with tiny white flowers in her hair, and her bridesmaids were dressed in yellow.'

The best man was a young doctor named David Moon. He and John had met in Darwin.

John went numb during the service, no doubt with nerves. 'Father Frank performed the ceremony, and I just remember standing there as proud as punch and feeling stupid, with this grin I couldn't take off my face.'

He and Anita glided down the aisle and time seemed to stand still. The happy couple were now Mr and Mrs John Cobby, with their shared life and dreams ahead of them.

John and Anita didn't have a honeymoon. It wasn't a priority. There was not really enough time, nor was there really enough money to have a proper getaway, and it didn't seem especially important. Instead the newlyweds moved out of the nurses' quarters, where they had spent their early months as lovers, and rented a small house in the Rockdale area as man and wife. Anita carried on nursing at Sydney Hospital, where she continued to be popular and well respected by the staff and her superiors. John worked at a variety of hospitals, mainly doing temporary nursing work, which was well paid.

With two good incomes, the pair were comfortably off. Theirs was a simple life, of going to work, attending the occasional concert, having dinners out; they continued to frequent The Prophet restaurant. There were weekends away at the snow, and also time spent regularly with each other's families. They each pursued their own interests: Anita had her drawing and John had his surfing and his horses. They bought two dogs: a Great Dane called Tiny and a kelpie called Lucy. 'Anita doted on those dogs, and would walk them constantly and cuddle them whenever she could,' John remembers.

They decided to buy a sailing boat – a twenty-four-foot Triton they purchased for $4500.

'We never got around to naming the boat,' John recalls, 'but we had it for two years and we spent some wonderful week-ends on it. Anita had never been into sailing, but she loved sitting on the deck with dogs.'

John loved the sea and, ever since he was a kid learning to sail at Yarra Bay Sailing Club in Sydney's east, he'd dreamed of owning a yacht. The couple spent weekends exploring the waters of southern Sydney with friends and family, taking the vessel from its mooring at Kogarah Bay, occasionally venturing into Sydney Harbour.

'Anita and I spent a week sailing up to Coffs Harbour soon after we bought it. We hugged the coast and then would spend the night in little ports we found. Her sitting on the deck with the dogs and me at the helm – just a magic trip.'

John's entire family had loved Anita from the moment they met her. His mother, Terri, had moved back in with her parents, bringing Gaynor with her. Anita and John's place was nearby and the newlyweds often visited.

Anita happily went there without John. She seemed to make time for everyone in that house at Rockdale: John's mother and sister, as well as his maternal grandfather, Da; his nanna, Stella; the cockatoo, who would swear and yell, 'Up the Rabbitohs'; and two dogs, Tiffy and Bessie. Where other young women would be intimidated by having so many family members around them at once, Anita took it all in her stride, embracing and loving them all without reservation.

But most of all, the pair enjoyed being alone together; it was all they really wanted.

CHAPTER 3

Travel, then the fork in the road

1985

As HAPPY AS THEY WERE IN SYDNEY surrounded by family and friends, John and Anita yearned for a change of scenery. John was keen to try his hand at training horses. He had a cousin, Alan Muggeridge, who could help him in Coffs Harbour, on the north coast of New South Wales, where the excellent beaches would also be a drawcard.

John wanted to make the move, and Anita was all for it. She supported him in anything he wanted to do, just as he supported her. Anita liked horses and was good with them, but saw them as pets. Still, she understood and respected the fact that for John they were a passion, as was surfing.

A mate built a special trailer for them that held everything, including the dogs, so they packed up and away they drove from Sydney in their little green Ford Escort. At first they lived in the outer suburb of Boambee; its beach and warm climate made it the perfect spot for a pair who loved the outdoors.

Husband and wife both landed jobs in a local private hospital. Once again, John began working night shifts, which gave him time to surf and train his horses by day. It was a dream come true for John. He found training and connecting with those magnificent beasts deeply satisfying. John's passion for horses had been with him since he was a child, with his mother's family involved in training horses for over a century. In his teenage years and early twenties, John would spend hours on the beaches of Monterey with trainer Terry O'Leary, a friend of his grandmother. Now he was living the dream of a horse trainer in the coastal town with three of his own horses: Kermansha, Pooka and Condle the Red.

When not working, Anita was devoted to her dogs. The couple socialised with John's cousin and a few friends, going to dinner or spending time around the country tracks of northern New South Wales, watching John's horses.

John and Anita's lifestyle was idyllic. John would take the horses down to the beach every day and run with them. While he was training, Anita would take the dogs for long walks along the beach. They were both healthy and in love. The miscarriage was behind them and the future was something they didn't really worry about.

For many months they drifted along in their north-coast paradise, largely oblivious to the rest of the world. After a while, they moved into the centre of Coffs Harbour to be closer to the racetrack and the hospital.

Anita's father would drop in from time to time on his way to Lightning Ridge, where he often went opal mining with a friend. He enjoyed getting right away from the city when he could. But his visits weren't always comfortable. The truth of the matter was that he and John didn't hit it off particularly well. Garry was a protective father and had never quite taken to the man who had stolen his daughter's heart; he thought she could do better. Nevertheless, he and John were civil for Anita's sake.

John and his horses were soon doing well. John was a lucky punter, although he stuck to his rule of only backing the horses he trained. He didn't bet all that often, but when he did he would bet pretty big. Anita had no objections to John's gambling, and in fact it brought about a huge windfall that would change their lives.

About a year after the couple arrived at Coffs, John had a particularly big win on one of his horses in a maiden race at Grafton. It was a 1200-metre race, and the horse, which was called Kermansha (by Marakesh), romped it in. Michael Souri, owner of The Prophet, had flown up from Sydney, and the two men placed a number of bets with the rails bookies. The horse came home at thirteen to two and John Cobby collected over $10,000 cash that day. It was a huge amount of money in 1985, especially for a couple with no debts or dependents.

Although buying a house might have been a sensible thing to do, they were young and adventurous and decided to head overseas instead. A few years earlier, when she was crowned Miss Western Suburbs, Anita had won a trip to Hawaii, which had whetted her appetite for travel. John had also enjoyed his surfing trips to Indonesia. Now they had the means to go as far as Europe, and they grabbed the opportunity with both hands.

It was Anita who was the driving force behind the trip. John's mindset was a lot more 'take it or leave it', but he freely acquiesced. Anita had backed him in the shift to Coffs Harbour and his move into training horses; now it was her turn, he figured – not that it was a sacrifice in any way. Plenty of their friends were travelling, many of them working in pubs and bars in America and England. Waves of young Australians were backpacking around Europe. Anita's enthusiasm was infectious, and John was quickly caught up in it.

Anita forced John out of his comfort zone. That was how their relationship worked. They weren't peas in a pod – more like different pieces of a puzzle that fitted together brilliantly.

*

Tingling with excitement, John and Anita took off from Sydney's Mascot airport. John was petrified of flying but Anita helped him stay calm. He had a drink to ease his nerves and she held his hand, and they set off on their big adventure.

First stop was the west coast of America. From the beaches of Coffs Harbour, the couple headed for the beaches of Los Angeles. It was like a belated honeymoon. They spent their days in a very relaxed way – walking along the sandy coastal strip taking in the sights and reading. There was one particular book shop they visited nearly every day. 'It was called the Buddha Tree,' John says. 'Anita was into self-help books and read *Jonathan Livingston Seagull* at that time.' John saw her as a beautiful soft seagull learning about life. Above all, they were journeying together – and it was forever.

Next they headed for New York, crossing America on a Greyhound bus, visiting places like Tombstone, Arizona, on the way. They were taking it all in and having a ball. For John, it was as though the two of them became one person during this holiday, seeing the world together. They didn't get on each other's nerves the entire time they were away.

But it was in Italy where their romance reached new heights. They got by with their little phrase book, stayed in small *pensioni*. Every day they drank red wine and ate cheese. In Rome they ticked off every romantic ritual they could, visiting destinations popular with lovers from all over the world.

The Trevi Fountain was a standout. They had spent days looking for it, but kept getting lost or else side-tracked by an unexpected sight or an amazing restaurant or café that took their fancy. When, finally, they stumbled upon it, they just said, 'Whoo, this is amazing.' Everything about Rome seemed so magical, so romantic.

They caught the train down to Bari then spent days in Brindisi at beachside cafés eating fresh fish before heading to Greece. The weather there was perfect. They drank lots of ouzo and went crazy over lamb shanks, which they dined on almost daily. One day, they went to a movie theatre to see *Amadeus*. It cracked them up when they discovered it was in English with Greek subtitles – so unexpected.

They had been travelling like there was no tomorrow, without a care in the world, spending money like confetti. The day came when they had to face the fact they were broke. They decided to borrow some money from family to keep going just a little longer. Anita, especially, was enjoying travelling so much. They were confident they would be able to pay it back. But eventually that too ran out and reluctantly they packed their bags.

It was mid-1985 when they returned to Australia. John recalls, 'Anita was restless. She made no secret of the fact that she hadn't wanted to come back, but recognised that we had no choice.'

They set up home in Arncliffe and tried to resume their old Sydney life, but Anita was still consumed with the travel bug and felt dissatisfied.

John didn't share her feelings. He had had his fill of travelling and was keen to settle down. He liked security, was heading towards thirty and was starting to think about a family.

But at that stage it was the last thing Anita wanted. And as time passed, her restlessness didn't go away. The magic spell they'd been under in Rome was broken. They were no longer two hearts beating as one but two people pulling in opposite directions.

There were no arguments about gambling. No affairs. No dramatic scenes. Just a need – mutually recognised – for some time out. It was a simple matter to arrange, so that was what they did.

CHAPTER 4

John and me

Monday 1 July 2013

A MAN GOING BY THE NAME OF JOHN FRANCIS is living quietly
in a flat near Bronte Beach. His is the top-floor apartment in
a small block of twelve. He bought it three years ago. It was
small and needed renovating, but it was close to the surf he
craved so much. While his body is fit and tanned from his years
at the beach, he is heavily tattooed and his face bears the lines
of daily battles with anger and a lack of self-worth.

It's the afternoon of 1 July. The phone rings, startling him.
He puts down his ever-present glass of red wine to take the call.
It's his sister. She breaks the news of the death of his former
mother-in-law. Anita Cobby's mother, Grace 'Peg' Lynch, has
passed away at the age of eighty-eight.

The siblings chat for a few minutes. Theirs is a close relationship. Thanking his sister for the heads-up, he places the
phone back in its charger. He now knows to avoid any news
sources – internet, newspapers, TV or radio – for the next
few days; no, he won't expose himself to anything that might
amplify his darkest memories.

John Francis sits down and picks up his glass. Time has little meaning. Thoughts, half-remembered events and powerful emotions flood through him.

He is deeply saddened by this news. Although he hasn't spoken to Peg in years, he has always admired her and knows how much Anita loved her. Mother and daughter were so close. John can see them even now, talking together and laughing at their own secret jokes. He remembers the day he and Anita were married and how kind Peg was as she gave him her blessing. He is plunged back into memories of happy times spent with both women, and night falls before he moves from his chair.

He promised to love and look after Anita forever. Those words haunt him to this day.

Even though the death of Grace Lynch came twenty-seven years after her daughter's murder and she had not been in the public eye since her husband Garry had died five years previously, the event was still newsworthy. Mrs Lynch had captured the hearts of the nation with her dignity in the midst of tragedy. While Garry had become the public face of Anita's grieving family, Grace had quietly stood behind him and was every bit as passionate an advocate for the victims of homicide, co-founding the support group of that name and campaigning tirelessly for it.

I was at work when I got a call telling me of Anita's mother's death, which I had been expecting. A few days beforehand I had been rung by a contact who had told me Grace Lynch was gravely ill and not expected to live.

When the inevitable news came through that Grace had passed away, it provoked a flurry of activity in the office. I quickly wrote a short story for the internet – now an integral part of every newsroom, though decades away when Anita was murdered. It made the availability of news almost instant, but a longer news feature was put together for the next day's edition of the *Daily Telegraph*, reminding the public of the evil that had walked the streets of Sydney almost three decades earlier. As well as going over the details of Anita's death, both articles talked about how Grace had lived up to her name in the way she had handled being in the glare of publicity.

It was obvious to me that her funeral at Pinegrove Cemetery, Minchinbury, would be attended by hundreds of people whose lives had been touched by the case. However, I would not be joining my fellow journalists, or the detectives, politicians and hordes of admirers, family and friends who were bound to attend. To be blunt, I had moved on, not to mention the fact that I was flat chat with work. The Hells Angels and Comancho bikie gangs were at war and Sydney was in the grip of a series of drive-by shootings.

The Cobby case and Grace's funeral were not high on my agenda that Monday night when my phone rang as I was getting ready to leave the office.

'Hello, Mark Morri speaking.'

'Hello, Mark,' came a soft voice at the other end of the phone. 'John Francis here. How are you?'

Instantly I realised I was speaking to the person I still thought of as John Cobby even though he always introduced himself as Francis. I'd know that voice anywhere. In 1987, I'd spent three days holed up in a hotel with him, taping him while he gave his account of his wife's murder to the *Mirror.*

By coincidence, years later, we'd ended up living close to each other in the eastern beaches area of Sydney. One day I had spotted him walking on Bronte Beach, and that afternoon had rung him for no real reason except to say hello. There was an immediate reconnection and we had remained in contact ever since, gradually becoming friends. I knew he trusted me. Above all, I understood his history.

Our get-togethers had a clear pattern: we used to sit and drink, and only then would John find his voice. The anger and hurt would come out. Otherwise, he was reclusive, a bird nursing a broken wing, trying to fly and not having much luck.

It would be years before we agreed that I should write this book. A tribute to Anita. His side of the story. He had been incapable of telling it all those years ago but now he was as ready as he'd ever be. It would never be an easy process for someone who, nearly thirty years later, was still dealing with the after-effects of the trauma he'd gone through.

Today, the pleasantries were dealt with in seconds. What John wanted to know was whether I thought there would be a lot of media interest in Peg's passing, as his sister Gaynor had suggested. Also, if I planned on going to the funeral, he suggested that the three of us could go together – John, Gaynor and me. (Gaynor is now a wedding celebrant, married with a child.)

I quickly scotched that idea. 'If you are with me, other journalists are going to ask questions. There could be people there who will recognise you.'

What I had yet to understand was how thorough John had been with his self-imposed media blackout. From the moment of Anita's murder, he had avoided any mention of the case – if there was ever a photo or a glimpse of the name Cobby, he'd throw down the paper like a hot potato; similarly, the TV or radio would be turned off quick smart, the website rapidly. Although it sounds implausible, he genuinely had no idea what strong feelings Anita's death aroused in Australia, and particularly Sydney, even after all this time.

When I tried to explain it to him, the thought of possibly being recognised as the husband of Anita scared him. 'Fuck that. I don't want that. Maybe I'd better stay away.'

It was obvious that he was torn, however. He told me that he considered Peg an amazing woman, and that he admired her strength and compassion.

After a few minutes of talking about Peg and how he was coping with life generally, which wasn't well, John seemed to agree that going to the funeral with me was not a sensible option. Peg and her second daughter, Kathryn, had always respected his desire to stay anonymous. He knew Peg would have understood, as would Kathryn, if he didn't attend the funeral.

But by the time our conversation came to a close, I was still unsure of his plans. Some days later I discovered that he *had* gone – with his daughter, Aerin, Gaynor and her husband, Peter.

'I had to. I couldn't stay away,' he explained to me. 'She was such an amazing woman and I wanted to be there.'

A miracle of sorts occurred that day. Peg was buried at the same cemetery as her husband and daughter. After the hordes had gone, and close family had departed for the wake, John Cobby went to the grave site of his late wife.

He had only been there once since Anita's funeral, and that was in 1997.

When he told me about the grave-site visit, I was surprised but felt stirrings of hope about John and his state of mind. Was it possible that after all this time locked in grief, this damaged, reclusive man was coming to terms with his harrowing loss?

CHAPTER 5

Missing . . . and found

Monday 3 February 1986

FOR FIFTEEN HOURS, THE ANITA COBBY CASE was a mundane missing person's report. Her father went to Blacktown police station with a photo of his daughter and reported her disappearance at 6.30 on the Monday evening. To police, the case appeared straightforward. Essentially, a young woman, recently separated from her husband, had failed to turn up at work earlier in the day. There were no alarms bells going off as the young police officer, Constable Murphy, took down the details from Garry Lynch.

Earlier that afternoon, Anita's superior at Sydney Hospital, Sister Jolly, had rung the family home to make sure Anita wasn't sick. Anita hadn't reported for her regular 1.30 pm shift. When she had not arrived for work or contacted anyone, Garry and his wife genuinely thought something bad must have happened to her. Their daughter would never let anyone down like that. Of course, they had been expecting her to come home on the Sunday night too. When she hadn't arrived, they assumed she had decided to stay with her friends, something she had done before.

It was a routine matter, commonplace at police stations all over the country, where over-anxious parents were quick to report their children missing, even though they were adults. The young woman would no doubt turn up; they invariably did.

Tuesday 4 February 1986

At 11.30 am, dairy farmer John Reen noticed something strange. His cows were milling around the corner of the part of his property known as 'the Boiler Paddock'. When actively grazing, cows tend to spread out. Earlier that morning, when he had passed that spot on his way to some cattle sales, the cows had been in the same patch. At that time, he hadn't thought anything of it. But when they were still there three hours later, he thought he'd better check it out.

The 43-year-old got on his motorbike to investigate what the cows were so curious about. What he discovered would haunt him for life.

In the paddock, lying on her stomach totally naked, was the body of a woman.

Reen raced to his house and phoned police. He reported that the body was slightly swollen and had obviously been lying there for some time. Within minutes, hordes of officers were crawling all over the Boiler Paddock.

In 1986, Reen Road, Prospect, could be described as semi-rural and fairly deserted. A narrow road which ended in a group of paddocks dotted with scattered clumps of trees, it was a well-known lovers' lane. Young couples from the surrounding suburbs – including Blacktown, 4 kilometres away – would often hang out there after dark.

To say that the character of the area has changed since

1986 is to put it mildly. Nowadays the area is semi-industrial and Reen Road doesn't exist. It has morphed into two separate streets: Peter Brock Drive and Auto Place. Developers have built sports and leisure facilities such as Eastern Creek Raceway, Eastern Creek International Karting Raceway and a Wet 'n' Wild leisure complex. There is now a fast-food outlet near where John Reen found Anita's body.

When police questioned the shocked farmer, they wanted to know if he'd seen or heard anything unusual. Reen told police he had been sleeping fitfully. It had been a hot few days, a typical start to the stifling humidity associated with February in Sydney. He remembered being woken late at night by the sound of screaming coming from the direction of Reen Road. It could have been either Saturday 1 or Sunday 2 February. But he put it quickly out of his mind and went back to sleep. Hearing loud noise in the vicinity was nothing unusual. Young people often congregated nearby to drink and party.

Following their interview with Reen, police filed this report:

About 11.30 am on the 4.2.86 a dairy farmer John Francis Reen of Monhaven, Reen Road, Blacktown, investigated an object on his property known as the 'Boiler' paddock.

This is a leased paddock from the Water Board where he grazes cattle. He had noticed an object about 11 am this date from the roadway when returning home to his property. His attention had been drawn to the area where he saw the object by his cattle milling in one area, which appeared to be unusual to him.

The body appeared to be that of a young female, completely naked and devoid of any means of identification other than three gold interlocking wedding rings on a finger on her right hand.

She was face down with her legs apart and there was obvious severe lacerations to the right side of her neck.

Mentions were also made in the report of various other lacerations the victim had suffered on both her hands and fingers, and to numerous abrasions on her back.

Even from this initial report of the injuries, the police knew they were dealing with a homicide of the worst kind.

After sealing off and photographing the crime scene, police removed the deceased's body around 6.00 pm and transferred it to the morgue at Westmead Hospital. By 6.30, medical examiner Dr Joseph Michael Malouf had filed a six-page autopsy report.

Nearly thirty years later, I read his now barely legible handwritten report. It began with the simple sentence 'The body is a woman of average build and average weight of 52 kilos, height 175 cm.' However, nothing else contained in Malouf's report could be described as average:

1) Lacerations: Particularly on the right side of her neck, was somewhat irregular. On the right-hand side of her neck, there was virtual complete destruction of tissues – muscles, nerves and arteries and veins – and the spinal column bones were depressed and the spinal canal entered in its upper extremity.

2) Abrasions: Over the upper and centre quadrant of the right breast – upper measured approx. 1 cm in diameter, the lower abrasion 2 cm by 1 cm.

3) Left hand: Defence wound on the outer part of the left hand, running down the outer edge of the middle finger, which measured 6 cms. Other lacerations running across the tops of the middle finger and the thumb.

Severe lacerations to the inner middle finger and the ring finger of the left hand, severely damaging the tendons on these fingers, and smaller superficial lacerations on the base of the left thumb top.

Right hand: No visible injuries.

Upper arms: Series of small abrasions and contusions of both upper arms. But more pronounced on the left upper arm.

Left shoulder: Number of small abrasions on left shoulder.

Right leg: A number of small lacerations extending along the length of the outer side of the right thigh and right leg.

Left leg: These lacerations similar to the type as the outer right thigh, except on the interior of the left thigh and leg.

Right knee: Small laceration on the front of right knee.

Right thigh: Series small lacerations on the right knee.

Right thigh: Small series of lacerations on the back of right thigh.

Back: Linear abrasions, 11 to 12 cms in length, posterior wall of the right chest, extending upwards and laterally from the midline about the centre of the chest.

A 5 cm abrasion on the left chest, 10 cms above abrasion above and parallel to it. Number of small abrasions over the vertebrae. Abrasions around the outer side of the right elbow.

Anus: The anus was dilated – up to 3 cms – with recent lacerations present up the anterior and verge.

Fly and larvae recovered and maggots up to 5 cm present, collected.

Cranial cavity: Removal of the scalp revealed multiple bruises with small haematomas present. The brain was soft. No evidence of severe haemorrhage. Petechial haemorrhage present. Maggots, up to 4 cm in length, present along the medulla and brain stem and in the 4th ventricle.

Thoracic cavity: Contusions between the 5th and 6th left ribs noticeable. The lungs were inflated.

Abdominal cavity: The abdomen and contents contained approx. 55 ml partially digested food of an aromatic nature. Meat and veg matter easily identifiable.

The report finished with the simple statement that the victim had bled to death: 'Direct cause of death: BLOOD LOSS (EXTERNAL) LACERATION OF THE NECK', Malouf wrote, his capital letters like a volley of punches.

The details were sickening. They painted a picture of repeated, vicious bashing. More revelations would soon follow. Australians would be spared nothing of the horror that had taken place in the Boiler Paddock.

Wednesday 5 February 1986

Once police pieced together the snippets of information, Anita Cobby's name was no longer attached to an unremarkable missing person report. As the public was about to discover, she was the tragic victim of the worst homicide Sydney had ever seen.

When the story got out, it was as though a keg of gunpowder had been ignited. Media outlets frantically reported on the murder, and the outpourings of emotion began. Soon the city was seething. A defenceless nurse walking home had been stripped naked, brutalised and murdered.

Photos of Anita started appearing everywhere. There was the one from 1979, when she'd been crowned Miss Western Suburbs and was photographed with Premier Neville Wran at a charity event. Another, taken just five days before her murder by a freelance photographer as she walked through Martin Place, showed a beautiful young woman with a radiant smile. These images reinforced the public's perception of a caring and totally innocent person killed for no reason.

Around the rest of the country there was a small ripple of interest. Back then the cities of Australia were much more parochial, preoccupied with events taking place in their own backyard. But that was about to change.

Friday 7 February 1986

Just three days had passed since the discovery of Anita's body when John Laws, the uncrowned King of Sydney Radio, did the unthinkable. Early that morning, he had received a fax detailing Anita's injuries. Because of the high profile of the case, New South Wales Police headquarters had asked to be copied in on every aspect of the murder and subsequent investigation. Even though the report was marked 'Confidential: For the eyes only of Assistant Commissioner Ross Nixon', someone in either the police department or the coroner's office took the decision to leak it to Laws.

Shortly after nine o'clock on his top-rating morning radio show, John Laws broke with protocol and read out large parts of the official, typed-up autopsy report from the medical examiner live to air.

Among other disturbing findings, John Laws revealed the following:

> The deceased suffered from a number of wounds to the neck which severed the carotid artery, trachea and oesophagus and spinal cord and apparently died from severe loss of blood from all three wounds. The neck injuries were so severe that the head was almost severed from the body. There was bruising and swelling to both eyes, consistent with having been punched, together with a number of bruises to the skull. An x-ray of the body will be taken on the 5.2.86 to establish whether both shoulders have been either dislocated or fractured. There were several other lacerations apparently caused by a knife to her face and multiple lacerations to both hands and fingers. Two fingers on the left hand were fractured and some joints almost severed. The body showed other signs of having been beaten, probably during a very violent struggle which Doctor Malouf considers has taken place prior to death.

Listeners' reactions were immediate and overwhelming. The switchboard went out of control, with callers both sickened and outraged at the description of the young woman's death. Senior police, including Police Commissioner John Avery, went on the warpath to find out who had leaked such sensitive and confidential details to Laws. The investigation quickly cleared the investigating officers on the case.

'We were appalled that we were even under suspicion,' says Ian Kennedy, still bristling with anger at the thought. 'The investigators had the fax Laws received and it was clear it did not come from any of the guys working on the case.'

'It was a big decision to read it out,' John Laws confesses to me in early 2015. 'I spent hours deciding whether I would or not. It was so graphic and quite distressing. But in the end I decided the public had a right to know what these bastards had done to her.'

A leading broadcaster for fifty years, Laws still believes the murder of Anita Cobby is one of the worst crimes he has ever known. He agrees with me that it was his reading of the autopsy report that catapulted a horrible murder into the national sphere.

'People were upset about the murder of this young woman but after they heard and became aware of the horrible details, it turned to rage. There were many parts I didn't read, though.

'I copped a lot of flak for what I did, including from Anita's father, Garry, who let it be known he was not happy.'

But a few years before he died in 2008, Garry Lynch got in touch with Laws. He had had a change of heart by then. 'I can't remember the exact year but he rang me and said I did the right thing, that it needed to be done.'

Regardless of how Laws had come by the information, most of Australia was now a lot better informed about what Anita had endured. An already outraged public and media went into overdrive. This was no ordinary murder. The victim had been made to suffer the most degrading sexual abuse, and had fought with such intensity her fingers were broken and her shoulders dislocated.

Inevitably, many Australians started calling for a return of the death penalty. People were frightened too. With a monster – or monsters – loose on the streets, no Sydneysider felt safe.

Speculation about what had happened to Anita soon gave rise to rumours that spread like wildfire through the city. That her breasts had been cut off. That she had been raped with a number of objects, including a bottle. Although no evidence was given in the trial or by the killers that objects had been used on Anita – and years later Detective Ian Kennedy told me that during the investigation there was never the slightest shred of any such evidence – those rumours persisted. The gossip mill was further fuelled by a police entry stating that samples of semen had been recovered from her vagina and anus, which had been severely torn. Another quote from the report was bandied around: 'The neck wound was so severe it prevented semen being detected in the mouth.' The details of the autopsy report were circulating by word of mouth among journalists throughout the city and did nothing but feed the atmosphere of fear and revulsion.

After the autopsy details hit the airwaves, and with the public baying for blood, the case could easily have become a political football. Premier Neville Wran got involved immediately and asked for day-to-day briefings and a copy of the autopsy report.

'He was too upset to read it after a page or two,' his then press secretary and now Channel Nine executive David Hurley revealed recently. 'Wran was no shrinking violet. He had been a lawyer for many years and was a pretty tough sort of person. He had seen a few things in his time but this really distressed him.'

'I just can't read it,' he said to David Hurley. 'These are acts so despicable. They are not the acts of a human being.'

There was even a personal connection. Not only had Neville Wran been photographed with Anita at the races in 1979 after she won her beauty pageant, but in a quirky coincidence, his daughter Kim had had an acting role as a nurse in the TV series *The Young Doctors* at the time.

A talented politician, he also recognised that his state – and perhaps, now, the whole country – was as deeply affected as him.

Wran moved swiftly. Within the week of the murder, he had put up a $50,000 reward for information leading to the arrest of the perpetrator or perpetrators. A few days later, he increased it to $100,000.

Offering a reward so quickly was unheard of. In most cases, it takes years before rewards are advertised, and then it happens only when every other investigative tool is exhausted. Police hadn't asked for the reward to be posted, but they were not about to object to anything that might give them a lead.

'Neville didn't make the decision out of political motivation,' Hurley tells me. 'This was different. Whoever had done this had to be taken off the streets.

'I had my own copy of the autopsy report and started reading it. I got to a point where, like the boss, I couldn't go on. I just put it down. These were acts of animals, like he said, not humans in any way.'

After the killers were caught, Garry and Grace Lynch visited the premier in his office. 'Neville was struggling for words,' says Hurley. 'He was a great politician and orator, but when he met the parents he didn't know what to say. He called out to me, "Son, come in here for second, please." He told me later he needed support, someone else to help him find words to fill the silence.'

Hurley and Wran were both impressed by the decency and dignity of the older couple, who had been subjected to having their daughter's ghastly final moments aired in public. 'Neville advised them not to go to the inquest or committal proceedings. He was talking not as a politician but as a father. He didn't think they should hear what he couldn't even read. It was a murder that took the city by storm.'

In the midst of all the media frenzy, and while the temperatures of February soared, at Blacktown police station it was all hands on deck. Just as the case had rocked politicians, the media and ordinary Australians, police too were disturbed. Homicide is always horrific in nature, but the brutality of the murder of Anita Cobby had rattled even the most seasoned members of the force.

There was a sense of urgency to find the murderer or murderers, to get them off the streets before they did something similar again – and to see them brought to justice.

CHAPTER 6

The investigation

Tuesday 4 February 1986

IT WAS SHORTLY AFTER LUNCH when Detective Sergeant Graham Rosetta of Blacktown police station answered a phone call at his Penrith home. It was always good to have a day off, and he was enjoying pottering around.

As soon as he heard the urgency in the voice at the other end of the phone, he switched straight back into work mode. His station boss, Sergeant First Class Tony Cassimatis, informed him that the body of a young woman had been found in a paddock. It sounded bad. Rosetta was told to drop everything and begin working on the case immediately.

Rosetta's partner, Detective Hugh Dundas, also had his leave cancelled. Dundas lived at Emu Plains, further away, so he drove past Detective Rosetta's place and picked him up.

At around 2.30 pm, Detectives Rosetta and Dundas, accompanied by medical examiner Dr Joseph Malouf, entered the Boiler Paddock. Police tape was erected around the crime scene. A number of scientific police were already in attendance and taking photographs.

When I interview Detective Rosetta for this book, he instantly recalls the moment he approached the spot where Anita's body lay. An image of what he saw became permanently etched in his mind. Nevertheless, he opts to refer to a copy of the notes he put down in his police diary: 'Reen Rd, Blacktown about 70m inside the fence is the body of a naked female, she is laying on her stomach, blood on both sides of her hands.' He noted the ground was well trodden, obviously from the cattle in the area, and observed that there were no houses in view.

What was not in his notebook was his gut reaction when he looked at the body. In death, Anita's eyes remained open, their expression frozen in time.

'The look in the girl's eyes I will never forget,' the retired detective tells me. 'Those dead eyes . . . you could see she had gone through hell. You could see it. She was only a small girl,' he adds, becoming emotional even all these years later.

Even without the scientific evidence that Dr Malouf would provide, Rosetta knew then and there that the extensive, heinous violence Anita had suffered was something that no person could have carried out alone. 'By looking at the body, I didn't think of a crime of passion at all. Instinctively, I knew she had been abducted by a group of some kind.'

Around the time Rosetta and Dundas were being summoned back to work, Detective Ian Kennedy was at his desk in the Homicide Squad, situated in the old Remington building in the heart of the city. It was close to 1 pm and Kennedy was about to go to lunch when he received a call informing him of the grisly discovery of a murder victim at Prospect. Although it is routine for the Homicide Squad to be notified immediately of any suspicious deaths, the investigation is often handled by local detectives for the first few days. In Australia, homicide is almost invariably a domestic matter. It is unusual for the expertise of trained homicide officers to be required in the initial stages of the police investigation.

Bookending the Cobby murder were two other high-profile homicides. Only days earlier, Kennedy's colleagues had been called to a house in Fairlight, where, in the early hours of 27 January, an intruder wielding a sawn-off shotgun had crept into the room where Megan Kalajzich and her husband, millionaire restaurateur Andrew Kalajzich, lay sleeping. The assailant had shot Mrs Kalajzich twice in the head and she had died of her wounds. Although her husband appeared to have had a narrow escape in a break-and-enter gone wrong, he would later be arrested. After a sensational trial, Kalajzich would be found to have become obsessed with another woman, then, desperate to be free to pursue his new love, to have taken out a contract with the hitman who ended his wife's life. He would be sentenced to life imprisonment. Released in 2012 after almost twenty-four years behind bars, Kalajzich would continue to protest his innocence.

On 6 February 1987, another attractive young woman would be found dead. Sydney prostitute and police informant Sally-Anne Huckstepp was floating in a duck pond when a park ranger came across her body early in the morning. Initially, drug over-dose was suspected. Twelve days later, it would emerge that the 31-year-old – girlfriend of a slain armed robber and heroin dealer named Warren Lanfranchi – had been strangled. Lanfranchi had been shot dead in 1981 by New South Wales's – if not Australia's – most famous detective, the now disgraced Roger Rogerson. (Years later I got to know Rogerson fairly well, and I covered his arrest for allegedly shooting a young drug dealer in 2015.) Soon after Lanfranchi's shooting, Huckstepp had embarked on a media campaign alleging her boyfriend had been set up by drug dealer Neddy Smith. This was never proven, and Huckstepp's murder remains unsolved to this day.

It was an intense period for Sydney's police force, especially the homicide team.

*

Detective Kennedy's regular partner was off duty when the call came through about the body found in Reen Road, Prospect. He grabbed two other detectives and was quickly on his way. Constable Garry Heskett and Senior Constable Kevin Raue both lived in the western suburbs, and Kennedy had a hunch that their local knowledge would be invaluable.

It took Detectives Kennedy, Heskett and Raue forty-five minutes to reach the spot where Anita's body had been discovered. All three found looking at the corpse every bit as confronting as had Detectives Rosetta and Dundas before them.

'It was a shocking sight, obviously,' Kennedy tells me. He goes quiet as he thinks back to the things he registered: the fact that the wedding ring on the right hand was the only piece of clothing or jewellery visible; that when Anita was moved, her head was barely attached to her body.

On viewing the corpse, Kennedy's heart sank. Straightaway his instincts told him this brutal killing would become a major media event. That was going to heighten the ordeal for the victim's loved ones; there would be no escaping the attention. Going by his experience, he knew he would be able to shield and advise them to a certain extent, but the lives of these people were about to be turned upside down.

Right now, though, he needed to figure out who they were. He and his colleagues were eager to put a name to the victim and begin the methodical work of solving the crime.

That turned out to be the quickest step in the entire investigation. Within minutes of checking the missing person's reports, police located the entry in the police message sheet from the previous evening when Garry Lynch had reported his daughter missing.

Next, Kennedy telephoned the family. On the basis of what was established during that conversation, Kennedy obtained the ring in its exhibit bag then made his way to the Lynches' home address, as listed on the missing person's report.

Garry, Grace and their 20-year-old daughter Kathryn were anxiously awaiting news of Anita when Kennedy knocked on the door. John was still driving up the coast in a daze.

When Kathryn immediately recognised the ring – as did John, who arrived shortly after Kennedy – the police were confident they knew the identity of the victim. But before they could state it as a certainty, an appropriate person had to make the formal identification. Within hours, that step too was complete.

While time stood still for the grieving family, detectives started work in earnest. Initially, their attention was on tracing Anita's last known movements. It didn't take them long to piece together the events of Sunday, Anita's last day alive. She had risen early and arrived promptly at Sydney Hospital in Macquarie Street, next to Parliament House in the city, where she worked a full shift on Ward 14.

Statements were obtained from her two friends and work colleagues Lyn Bradshaw and Elaine Bray. The running sheet summarises the information they provided to police:

On Sunday 2.2.86 the three commenced work at Sydney Hospital at 7 am and concluded their shift at 3.30 pm. And then remained in the visitor's room, where they chatted and drank coffee.

About 5.15 pm the deceased changed from her nurse's uniform into: A pair of red and white vertical striped jeans, white linen sleeved top with three buttons at the neck, a thick black belt leather with a round silver buckle, a pair of light brown moccasin-type slip-on shoes, size 6 and a half, and a Russian gold interlocking wedding ring consisting of three rings, on her right hand. She was carrying a black 'tote' bag, corduroy with gold or brown trim and large straps as a shoulder bag. Inside the bag she carried her maroon/brown folding wallet, which contained a small sum of money and personal papers. It is possible that the bag also contained all or part of her nurse's uniform and other clothing.

The three young women had hardly a care in the world as they then headed to Surry Hills to Azzars' Lebanese restaurant in Cleveland Street, not far from The Prophet, where John and his friend Sue would meet up with Noel Cobby the following evening, Monday 3 February.

According to the running sheet, 'There the three dined and consumed two bottles of wine between the three of them.'

It was about 8.30 pm when the women paid the bill and left. Night was falling. Lyn Bradshaw drove Anita to the Eddy Street entrance of Central railway station, less than a kilometre from the restaurant:

Bradshaw estimates the time she dropped the deceased off at the station as being just prior to 9 pm. (THIS IS NOT A DEFINITE – JUST AN ESTIMATION.)

This is the last that either Bradshaw or Bray saw the deceased alive.

That night with his family, Kennedy had a lot of trouble distancing himself from his job. There was a lot going on at home: he and his wife had a six-month-old son, Matthew. Matthew's early life had been difficult at times, as he had been born with bowel complications.

Over the course of the previous several hours, Kennedy had seen the body of a young female murder victim, tracked down and informed her family, then taken the father to the morgue and returned him home. As well, he had interviewed the grieving husband, asking him if he had anything to do with the murder. Remaining with the victim's family for the next while, he and his colleague had done their utmost to help them through those first torturous hours of grief. As was their professional duty, the pair had also explained to them, when the right moment arose, how vital it was that they mention to police any information that might be pertinent to Anita's murder, no matter how small or irrelevant they thought it was. Anything could help.

Detective Kennedy reinforced to Garry that there was going to be a lot of media attention surrounding his daughter's death, and asked him to do as much publicity as he could cope with.

Recently I was able to talk through with Speed Kennedy the events of February 1986. I have stayed in touch with him ever since the murder, as I have (off and on) with John Cobby (Francis). He explained to me, 'We needed the public to help, and the family were the obvious way that was going to happen. It turned out the Lynches were just incredible in the way they handled the glare of the media. [They] were incredibly strong and did everything we asked of them and then more. Garry did most of the talking and, while he seemed to be handling it very well, privately there were times he would break down.'

There's a saying that behind every great man there's a great woman, and that appears to have been the case with the Lynches. Continues Kennedy, 'There was one time when it was all getting to Garry, and Peg said to him, "We have to be strong for Anita."'

The big former detective pauses. 'No one should underestimate Grace's fortitude. She was a rock for him and has my undying admiration.'

It was painfully obvious that John Cobby was in no shape, nor did he have any desire, to take part in fronting the press. The only memory he has kept from that first day is of being completely blindsided by grief. Today, he is unable even to tell me where he was. He has a vague recollection that the family moved him to a friend's house to keep him away from the media.

Leaving the family to grieve, the detectives left O'Sullivan

Street and went back to Blacktown police station. There, it was all systems go. Already, a team of over twenty officers had been assembled. All were working furiously, combing through the facts so far assembled and trying to see if they could find any leads. The New South Wales Police hierarchy had let it be known that they didn't care about how much overtime was incurred, or how high the head count of the team. The killer or killers had to be taken off the streets at all costs.

'Almost from the moment the body was found,' Kennedy tells me, 'we were reporting to the head of Homicide, Ken Webster, who in turn was briefing the head of the CIB [Criminal Investigation Bureau], Superintendent Ron Stevenson.'

As mentioned, the briefings were soon being copied to Premier Neville Wran himself.

By 10.30 that night, investigators had received the autopsy report. It told them in medical terms what their eyes had already taken in and guessed at. The search to find out who could have done this horrendous act was already in full swing.

Tuesday 4 to Thursday 6 February 1986

While police had established that Anita was alive and in the city at about nine in the evening, they could not be positive she had caught the train home to Blacktown as she had intended. Where had she gone? Had she caught a cab somewhere else or met someone she knew? Every possible scenario about how Anita had ended up in the paddock was discussed. Police had been assured by Anita's family and her fellow nurses that she was a reliable and sensible person who would not have gone off with a stranger.

A rookie constable by the name of Paul Davies happened to have been working on the Monday night when Garry Lynch had reported his daughter missing. By a strange twist of fate, the young man had gone to the same school as Anita, Evans High at Blacktown, and at the same time. Perhaps it was this that prompted him to use his initiative.

Near midnight on the day Anita was found, Davies took it upon himself to check the message sheets – the notes taken from the police station's recent phone calls. And that was when he made the first real breakthrough in the case:

That . . . at 9.49 pm the Sunday at Probationary Constable ML Brown Telephone Message number 2/123. A call from Mr McGaughey of 87 Newton Rd [Blacktown], requesting see police about a suspicious car. Sergeant 2/class Malony attended and spoke.

Mr McGaughey said he and his sister Linda heard screams, looked outside, said it appeared girl was forced into a grey Holden which drove south along Walters Rd.

Police patrolled – no result.

What Constable Davies had turned up was this: the 123rd entry on the blotter at the police station was about the follow-up to a phone call received on Sunday 2 February, at the front desk from residents of Newton Road. They had heard some extremely disturbing screams from a woman, who appeared to have been pushed into a car against her will. Two officers had driven to Newton Road, but by the time they got there it was too late. The screaming woman and the car were gone, and the two officers had no real evidence that a crime had taken place. One of the two officers, Sergeant Malony, had written the brief report, stating that there had been nothing unusual to observe.

In 1986, police messages were typed on sheets and then stapled together for senior officers to study at the end of shifts. They were often brief and typed two-fingered by police officers who had spent hours on duty. Unbeknown at this stage to

Davies or any of his colleagues, Sergeant Malony's businesslike, six-line entry contained the basic details of Anita's abduction. Afterwards, once all the pieces of the puzzle were put together, Ian Kennedy would declare that the young police officer's initiative to check the logs had saved hours and hours of police work.

Davies's finding didn't yield much that police could use straightaway. All Malony had been given was a vague description of a Holden sedan, possibly an HG or HT model, white with a grey undercoat. Still, even if the screams turned out to have had nothing to do with Anita's murder, it was the most promising lead anyone had come across so far.

Within minutes of finding the entry, members of the police task force raced out to Newton Road and arrived at the home of the McGaughey family, which included siblings Linda, John and Paul. The fact that it was already past midnight did not concern police. It was too serious a case to worry about a matter like waking and scaring an entire household. Most of the detectives had started work at around eight o'clock that morning, then been deployed to this task force. They were in a hurry: the longer it took for them to figure out who had committed the crime, the greater the possibility that the perpetrator/s would evade justice, maybe even strike again.

It was John McGaughey, aged 13, who had made the phone call to Blacktown police station on the Sunday night. He and Linda, his 14-year-old sister, had heard disturbing screams and had run out into the street.

When questioned by the task force, Linda told them she had seen a dark-haired woman being dragged into a car screaming and trying to break free.

Police recorded this note of the conversation:

She heard screams and saw a dirty white car. A man was pulling a female into the rear seat by her arm and she called out to her brother.

He ran towards the vehicle and as he did the rear door closed and drove off.

Concerned, the two young teenagers had phoned the police station immediately and made their report.

Could this be the genuine lead that police had been hoping for?

Certainly, when they then spoke to John and Linda's elder brother Paul it started to seem that way. He and his girlfriend, Lorraine, had narrowly missed the drama. When they arrived home minutes later, something about the conversation he had with his brother and younger sister made Paul and Lorraine decide to drive around to see if they could spot the Holden. The first place the couple chose to look was Reen Road – the well-known park-up spot.

Here is the record of the conversation police had with Paul, presumably having roused him from his sleep in the early hours of Wednesday morning:

About 1 am 5/2/86 Police attended the premises of 87 Newton Road, Blacktown and there spoke to Paul Francis McGaughey, 21, of that address and spoke to Brigid Lorraine Busher.

On the 2/2/86 both persons were at 87 Newton Rd Blacktown when they had a conversation with John McGaughey in relation to a white coloured Holden sedan with grey undercoat thereon. John McGaughey apparently heard screams coming from the street and it appeared that a girl was being forced into this vehicle. Paul McGaughey and Busher then went for a drive to Reen Rd, Prospect and there saw a red coloured Sigma Scorpion car parked on the left hand side of the road, a bit further along saw a 1970 Holden parked on the right side of the road, this car had grey primer paint. No person was seen in the vehicle.

It appeared to be similar to the one described to him by his brother.

About 9.30 pm on the 4/2/86 both McG and Busher were in Main street Blacktown when they saw a similar car to that seen on the 2/2/86. This vehicle was followed by McGaughey in Flushcombe Road then past Westpoint and the number of the vehicle being KEJ 554. When the vehicle was seen there were four males in the vehicle with two in the front and two in the back.

The Sigma parked in Reen Road and the Holden that the couple followed two days later turned out to be false leads. Nevertheless, other neighbours of the McGaugheys provided police with almost identical stories of hearing screams on the night Anita was murdered.

Across from the McGaugheys at 94 Newton Road, Lorraine Delauney and her son, Steven Hobson, were watching TV in their loungeroom when at about 9.45 pm Mrs Delauney told police she heard a 'bloodcurdling scream' which sounded like a terrified female and seemed to be coming from directly outside her home.

She and her son went running outside – Steven in his pyjamas – and saw an off-white to grey vehicle with its lights off speeding away down Newton Road. Sixteen-year-old Steven told police he thought the dirty-looking car was an HJ Holden and had two people in it, although he couldn't be sure:

As the car accelerated away I saw a fellow run out from across the road and he said, 'A girl has just been picked up by two guys in that car.'

I said, 'That car just going up there then?'

He said, 'Yes.' At this time I saw my next-door neighbour and I went back inside and got my shorts on and I drove with him and his girlfriend around the area, looking for the car for about ten minutes. We then returned home.

A woman at 96 Newton Road, Salne Midal Duin, who was visiting her aunty, told investigators a similar story. She said she had seen a girl being forced into a dirty white Holden by three men. 'There were two males in the rear punching her as she screamed,' she added.

It couldn't be a coincidence that at around the same time four people in Newton Road had heard screaming coming from a woman being dragged into a car. And their descriptions of the car were remarkably similar.

As promising as it all seemed, police couldn't be absolutely certain that the woman in the car was Anita. They were still not sure she had been in the area. Consequently, they continued following all lines of inquiry, covering all bases. Tips – most of which were found to be unrelated to the crime – were pouring in. Police were receiving hundreds upon hundreds of calls from all sections of the public, ranging from well-meaning citizens, to malicious types out to make trouble, to the downright crazy, and more than a couple of clairvoyants. Any known sex offenders in the area were rounded up and interviewed, and their alibis had to be carefully checked. No stone was to be left unturned.

The investigators had to steel themselves for the leads that went nowhere, the lines of inquiry that petered out, the myriad ways in which their hopes were raised only to be dashed.

The first such incident happened forty minutes after the discovery of the body. Police got excited when they were told there was an occupied car parked adjacent to where the body had been found. A man was sitting in his Toyota sedan, which seemed suspicious. When police searched his car, their hearts started racing. In the boot they discovered a sheaf for a kitchen knife, hedge cutters, a tomahawk and a spade.

The occupant of the car was taken back to the station for questioning. He told police he was a storeman for the Department of Education. At 8.30 am that day, when he had arrived at work, he had found out that the union had pulled a strike, so he'd had to make himself scarce. Rather than go home – believing that his wife would be furious at him for having the day off – he decided to park for a while and let time go quietly by.

Police rang his wife and workplace and the story was quickly verified. It was also noted that the man had no criminal record of any kind.

There seemed to be no end of similar cases. Suspects were coming thick and fast as the public inundated the police phone lines with 'information'.

In the course of the investigation, a small but important detail emerged that helped police understand what options Anita would have faced if she had caught the train back to Blacktown. There was a bank of public telephones at Blacktown railway station. On the night of 2 February, none were working – they had all been vandalised – making it impossible for Anita to ring her dad and ask him to come and collect her. Had she arrived at Blacktown station and decided to walk the 2 kilometres home? Or had she hailed a cab? For a while police were entertaining the possibility that a taxi driver might have been involved. Could Anita have jumped in with a cabbie who then took advantage of a lone, attractive woman sitting in his taxi late at night?

'There was some talk around that time that a cabbie was possibly involved in some sexual assaults, so it all had to be checked out,' Kennedy explains to me.

In the course of investigating this lead, police obtained the shift records of the drivers working for Western District Cabs at the time – seventeen in all. They also visited the rank at Blacktown railway station over the next few nights and interviewed many of the drivers personally, without any luck. They ruled out that possibility and forged on with other aspects of their painstaking work.

Various other possibilities were explored. Various scenarios were imagined. Every line of investigation was like an arrow being thrown into the air. The hope was that, sooner or later, one would hit the target.

My editor at the *Daily Mirror* had assigned me to the case. I was one of at least six reporters from the paper sent out to research stories connected with the murder. The instructions were clear from the bosses at work: keep the story alive by any means possible.

I was single, full of energy, and keen to impress the bosses. I'd start at 5 am and would be sent out to Blacktown police station or to the Lynch home to see if anything was happening. At night I would head to the pubs in Kings Cross and in the city near Sydney Hospital, on the off-chance that I might find some of her friends drinking there after work. Other reporters were camped at the police station overnight waiting for an arrest, or trying to catch a detective as he walked out of the station and perhaps get new information on how the investigation was going.

In the afternoon after Anita's body had been found, I went out to Blacktown railway station after spending the morning in the city trying without success to find nursing friends of Anita. I remember there were about a dozen public phones in and around the station and my boss had asked me to check them out. As investigators also discovered, all of them were out of order. Most of the receivers had been ripped off.

Garry later told police that Anita would probably have thought nothing of walking the 2 kilometres home on a warm night, especially if she couldn't ring him. There was close to zero per cent chance she would have bothered with a taxi. She loved walking.

At this stage I had no sense of who John Cobby was. His name was never mentioned by police. All they were saying was that Anita had been married and was now separated. They didn't elaborate publicly or privately, even to journalists they trusted.

What I know now is that, reeling from shock, John was staying out of sight, incapable of grasping the reality of what had happened let alone facing questioning from ravenous reporters desperate for information about his relationship with Anita. He tells me that, to this day, he doesn't understand how Garry Lynch could have been so calm and fronted the press on a daily basis. He suspects also that Garry didn't want John acknowledged publicly as Anita's husband.

Day in, day out, the Lynches put on a brave face in front of the public, but meanwhile John Cobby was going to pieces. As well as being overwhelmed by feelings of shock, grief and horror, he was plagued by paranoia.

Knowing what we do now, perhaps he had good reason to fear he was still a 'person of interest' in the criminal investigation. Detectives working on the ground level of the investigation had ruled John out as the killer early on, but perhaps not everyone was convinced. Occasionally the task force received left-of-field messages, including this one forwarded on by one of the state's then top cops:

6/2/86:

About 3.10 pm this date received a phone call from Assistant Commissioner Stirton from police headquarters – said he just received a phone call from a male, he believed to be a policeman or ex policeman from his manner of speaking.

'I won't tell you my name or how I know you but want to tell you, that the only person who could have murdered the woman at Blacktown was the husband. I have known the family a long time and I am a close friend.'

John breaks into an ugly smile when I tell him about this entry. 'I told you everyone blames the husband.'

But there was more. The night Anita's murder became public knowledge, another call came in to Blacktown police station and a short entry was made about 11 pm:

'I am a work colleague of John's. I've heard the things he had said about his wife – that he and several associates said. It should be checked out,' was all the anonymous caller said before hanging up.

Hearing this some thirty years on, John understandably seethes with anger. If I look at it from his point of view, I can only sympathise with him. It was a low act to say such vicious and downright libellous things. How cowardly and cruel to make such an allegation – while John was all but dying of grief – to provide no evidence to back up the statements and to phone in anonymously. In short, it was a gutless thing to do.

There was also the matter of the damning pronouncements made by Anita's two nursing colleagues. Lyn Bradshaw and Elaine Bray had painted a picture of John as a somewhat obsessive, maybe even angry person, unable to accept the finality of the split.

John argues vehemently against what the nurses told the police. 'We were getting back together again as clear as day. What she told them, I don't know.'

His sister Gaynor, to whom I spoke at length for this book, also says the reconciliation was beyond doubt. 'She had her wedding ring on when she died. That says a lot to me, plus the way she spoke about John.'

Everyone has their own truth. After the frightening 4 February interview with police, John Cobby was sure he was their number one suspect.

What I've found out since is that Kennedy's instincts told him that the man who had balled up into a crumpled wreck in the interview room was not a killer. No one could be that good an actor. To Kennedy, John Cobby was exactly what he appeared to be: a man robbed of the love of his life.

Wednesday 5 February 1986

At 11.10 pm on the Wednesday, a day into the investigation, a distraught husband and wife entered Blacktown police station with a story that bore some striking similarities to what police knew of the murder of Anita.

The woman, aged thirty, told police that she was walking from her home to a neighbour's house in Railway Parade, Quakers Hill, earlier that evening when a white or cream van with a group of males inside pulled up and the occupants tried to strike up a conversation with her. She was then dragged into the van and driven to a paddock – somewhere in Blacktown, she thought. There, a number of tablets were forced down her throat and she was made to smoke a cigarette. Then, the woman continued, she was dragged from the van and pushed down onto some grass, whereupon they tried to rip her clothes off. The last thing she remembered before she lost consciousness was scratching at their faces.

The woman said she had no idea how long she was unconscious, but as she started to come to, she heard one of the men ask whose turn it was and another say, 'I think she is dead.'

While her attackers were huddled in a group talking about her, the victim managed to grab her clothing. She then ran into some nearby bushes and somehow made it back to her home address, arriving there just as her husband was reversing out of the driveway to start searching for her.

On hearing what had happened, the man immediately took his wife to the police station to report the alleged attack. After taking down both their statements, the officers told the man to get his wife to the hospital and they would attend later. Police noted the victim did not appear to be affected by alcohol but seemed vague and perhaps sedated.

At 4.30 am, police rang the hospital, where the victim had been admitted to the women's surgical ward. A Sister Robertson informed police that the woman had begun to fit and appeared to be in a state of shock. She was treated for pain to her ribs, lower abdomen and for a few abrasions on her neck and arms. A social worker was also called in to talk to the woman and her husband.

'She refused to have a medical examination. Both she and her husband stated that should sexual intercourse have taken place, they preferred not to know about it.'

Could this have been another attack – within twenty-four hours – by the killers of Anita Cobby? Although there were frightening similarities, police suspected something was not quite right, that there was more to the story, when the pair refused to let the woman be examined. But detectives quickly established that her story was not linked to Anita's abduction.

On the running sheet of the Quakers Hill attack, which I viewed for this book, a two-page entry aroused my curiosity. The head of the Internal Affairs Unit, Superintendent Tony Sheppard, contacted the squad saying a woman had nominated a former Bandido bikie as a likely suspect.

I instantly recognised the name of the man whom the woman had accused.

Two years before Anita's death, Sydney had been rocked by what became known as the Milperra or Father's Day Massacre. Seven people died during a bloody shoot-out in the car park of the Milperra Hotel between the warring Bandido and Comanchero bikie gangs.

The star witness for the Crown – testifying against his fellow bikies in the subsequent court case – was codenamed WP. This was the person the woman had nominated as the potential leader of the attack against the 30-year-old woman snatched from the street in Quakers Hill. He was then – and remains – in a protected witness program and can't be named.

According to Sheppard, the female informant said that the bikie WP and an associate of his called Rolf were known to frequent the Reen Road area. She further alleged that WP was known to have been involved in violent sexual acts.

There was no follow-up entry in the running sheet, and after thirty-odd years, many of the documents from the investigation have gone missing. But it appears the woman's story came to nothing, as the detectives now have no recollection of the case.

'It must have been discounted in some way pretty quickly,' comments Graham Rosetta. 'I don't ever remember hearing about it and I think I would have remembered if it had any inkling of being related to the Cobby case.'

Like the vast majority of leads that came in the first week of the investigation, this one went nowhere.

Friday 7 to Sunday 9 February 1986

During those first few days of the investigation, members of the task force worked around the clock following up leads, as well as digging into Anita's personal life and checking John's alibi. Determined to find the killers, investigators were working ridiculous hours, often sleeping in the office and neglecting their families. As alibis checked out, leads were discounted and still no genuine headway was made, a sense of frustration inevitably crept in. But these were hardened professionals. They simply looked for new angles and ploughed on.

They were now reasonably certain of two things. Anita had caught the train from Central railway station and had been abducted by a group of men in Newton Road, Blacktown, as she began the walk back to her parents' place.

One of the lingering questions had to do with timing. The earliest train Anita could have caught to Blacktown if she had arrived at Central at 9 pm was the 9.12. If Anita *had* caught this train, she could not have been on Newton Road at the time when so many people heard the screams. Even though no one was exactly sure which train she *had* caught, they continued to work with the two assumptions mentioned above.

In one of their late-night brainstorming sessions – which often took place over a few beers or as they drove home together – Detectives Graham Rosetta and Kevin Raue came up with a fresh idea. Why not publicly re-enact those last known movements of Anita after she was dropped off at Central railway station? Perhaps that would jog people's memories, prompting individuals who might be holding on to information to come forward.

As the idea started to take form, the detectives realised they would need someone physically similar to Anita in order for the re-enactment to have any authenticity. A young probationary constable named Debbie Wallace, who was working at Blacktown police station, seemed the obvious choice. Wallace was about the same age and build as the slain nurse. Graham Rosetta thought she was perfect for the job. The rookie officer was honoured when she was asked to be involved.

On the Friday, Constable Wallace went shopping with Elaine Bray, who had dined with Anita on the Sunday night. They went to clothing stores all over the city looking for exactly the same clothing Anita had been wearing that night.

'Later it became a bit of a bone of contention that the clothes, particularly the pants I was wearing, were too tight-fitting and provocative, but it was the fashion of the day and not really that daring for the time,' Wallace tells me when I seek her out.

Anita's mother, Grace, was particularly annoyed, and made it widely known that her daughter was always modest in her attire and never wore anything tight-fitting or provocative.

'I wasn't really prepared for the impact the recreation would have and the amount of media attention it would draw,' says Detective Superintendent Debbie Wallace, now head of the New South Wales Gangs Squad and one of the state's most senior police officers.

The re-enactment started at Central railway station on the night of Sunday 9 February, exactly seven days after Anita had caught the train. Photographers and camera crews were allowed to follow the attractive young policewoman as she boarded the 9.12 train then sat in the carriage Anita had probably been on. It later turned out that Anita had in fact caught the 8.48 train, which put her at Blacktown at the time witnesses saw and heard her being bundled into the car.

As Constable Wallace sat on the train with cameramen photographing and filming her, detectives went through the carriages of the single-deck train, colloquially known as a 'red rattler', asking passengers if they had been on the same train the week before and, if so, whether they had seen anything suspicious.

At Blacktown, the media were asked to stand back, and Debbie Wallace spent the next twenty-five minutes walking down Newton Road and along other parts of the route police believed Anita would have taken to get home.

'It was quiet and eerie walking in her footsteps towards what we knew were most likely her last moments of feeling a young woman strolling on a summer's night, not worrying about anything. It was not a nice feeling,' Wallace confides to me.

The re-enactment got the media saturation the police were after, but unfortunately resulted in no new leads. By contrast, the impact on Debbie Wallace's own career proved to be enormous. Having walked in the steps of Anita, she felt some form of attachment to the investigation. She asked to be kept on the case and was granted her wish. It was what drove her to become a detective.

'I didn't do a lot, really. Mainly driving detectives around and getting lots of coffee, but I was part of the investigation, which is all I wanted – just to be part of a team trying to catch her killers.'

Her contact with the Lynches was minimal in the early stages of the investigation. 'I saw them at court during the trial but was really too embarrassed to approach them or invade their grief.'

Then, in 2003, in what many people thought was quite a bizarre event, the Casula Powerhouse Arts Centre decided to hold an exhibition centred on the death of Anita. Debbie Wallace was invited to be part of the quality-control board to make sure that the exhibits and the tone of the presentation were tasteful. 'Even though I thought it was an odd thing for an arts centre to do, I agreed to help out.'

The exhibition took place at Penrith later in 2003. Wallace tells me she will never forget the opening day.

'It was at the arts centre on the banks of the Nepean River. As I walked in through the door, Grace and Garry Lynch stood up and walked straight over to me.'

Garry grabbed the policewoman's hand, squeezed it and said, 'We have missed you. Come with us.'

Grace Lynch hugged Wallace and then asked her to sit next to them throughout the opening presentation and speeches. 'She never let go of my hand. It was really moving.'

From that day on, the Lynches and Debbie Wallace – the police officer who had played their daughter seventeen years previously – formed a special relationship. She was to spend hours with the couple and developed a particular bond with Grace Lynch.

'I remember Garry saying to me how aptly Grace was named.'

'So deep and quiet, as graceful as a lake,' he would say, referring to her tranquillity and strength.

Debbie shared many lunches with Grace over the years. 'What an amazing woman. Even when she was in palliative care, she never complained, talked about her woes or said anything untoward. It was all about how was I, how was so and so. Not about her situation. It was always about other people.'

To this day, the Cobby case is entrenched in Debbie Wallace's soul. 'I suppose you could say it changed my life.' She keeps in contact with Anita's sister and attended the funerals of both Garry and Grace.

It was the day after her re-enactment that another funeral took place.

CHAPTER 7

Saying goodbye

Monday 10 February 1986

SIX DAYS AFTER ANITA COBBY'S BODY had been found dumped in a cow paddock, the funeral of the caring, 26-year-old nurse with the impish sense of humour was held at Pinegrove Cemetery in Sydney's western suburbs, not far from where she had been murdered. Predictably, media were there in force, although I spent the day outside Sydney Hospital as more senior journalists covered the funeral.

The friends and family who gathered to mourn and to celebrate Anita's brief life were joined by hundreds of onlookers. The city was touched by the loss of this angel, snatched from the streets and brutalised. Fellow nurses from Sydney Hospital formed an honour guard as Anita's coffin, bedecked with flowers, was carried in for the service.

Uniting Church minister Reverend Keith Sweeting spoke of the life of Anita, her love of family and newfound passion for painting – something she had taken up in the last year of her life; she had always enjoyed drawing. Garry and Grace Lynch remained composed and stoic throughout. Many others broke down and openly wept.

Somehow John Cobby's family and police kept him out of the spotlight, slipping him quietly into a pew. Flanked by his sister, mother, father and a few close friends, he might have been present in body, but his mind was not fully there. Grief-stricken beyond description, John had been looking in all the wrong places for ways to deal with his pain.

'To be honest, the funeral was a blur,' he tells me. 'I think I had some heroin that morning and other sedatives. I had my first taste [of heroin] just three days after Anita was murdered. Until then I had never been into drugs. Not even dope; I'd tried it and didn't think much of it. But I wanted to hurt, to die, but didn't have the guts to outright kill myself.'

His father was tough on him, exacerbating their already strained relationship. On the day of the funeral, Noel Cobby said matter-of-factly, 'It's done now, get over it. You can't bring her back.'

Gaynor was her brother's rock from the day Anita disappeared, and she can't hide her emotion when she thinks back to the funeral. 'Dad was kind of holding John up in the church. Then John began screaming, "Don't take her away from me! Please don't take her away!"'

And – like his father-in-law six days before when he saw Anita's body in Westmead morgue – John's legs buckled. He had to be dragged outside by his father and a friend.

'It was so horrible, gut-wrenching. I can still see him now,' says Gaynor, fighting back tears as John's screaming still resonates in her memory.

John says he calmed down a little after that but stayed outside the church. He knows he was feeling wobbly, but not a lot else comes back except for the impression of a sea of people and the agonising pain and sense of loss.

In many ways, John Cobby was a ghost-like figure at the time, with his blond hair and his abstracted air. The Lynches had become the public face of the Anita Cobby murder inquiry. Although it seems like such a central topic, the marriage was almost totally ignored by the media. Questions about it were few and far between; on the one or two occasions when they were asked during a press conference, the answers given were brief and vague, and for some unknown reason – perhaps not wishing to risk exposing more pain when it was such a desperately tragic situation already – no one pressed the subject. It was treated as a thing of the past, almost irrelevant. No one asked why Anita had a different name from Garry and Grace. John's name rarely came up at press conferences. All that was said was that Anita and John had been separated and he was not part of the inquiry.

Privately it was intimated that detectives like Ian Kennedy and others on the case were telling the journalists not to pursue the topic of the husband. No real reasons were given, but because of their strong relationship with many of the journalists, this suggestion was respected and the matter was never widely pursued.

Even nowadays most members of the public are unaware that Anita was married, and certainly few at the time had any idea the couple had separated barely six weeks before the murder – or had spoken on the day she died.

In the tough days immediately following Anita's death, John had hidden away from the public at a house near Five Dock that belonged to one of his father's friends in the racing game.

'There was a stable hand's sister who came over. I knew she was into some pretty heavy things, and I asked her about getting some heroin for me. It was a totally impulsive act.

'It was just days after Anita was murdered and I have this memory. The house was near the water. And we snorted it or something like that the first time . . . I was taking Valium as well, I think. I just wanted to lie down and die. Go to sleep and never wake up.'

By the time of Anita's funeral, he had progressed to injecting heroin and travelling to Kings Cross with the strapper's sister to score in the seedy back streets. In the space of a week, John Cobby, previously a fit young man with a bright future, had not only become a widower but was on the verge of becoming a full-blown junkie.

The Cobbys felt something needed to be done about John, and it was decided the best thing was to get him out of the country, away from those few persistent journalists who wanted to pry into his personal life. John's father spoke to Detective Kennedy, who gave him the okay for John to leave Australia. The cops were now sure John hadn't done it, regardless of how paranoid and guilty he felt himself.

Plans were hatched to send John to Michigan in the US, where an old schoolfriend called Steven – now a psychologist – had offered to look after him and help him with his grief. Gaynor, Noel and Terri Cobby and a handful of close friends were at the airport to see him off.

'I was scared, grief-stricken and really didn't know what was going on,' recalls John. 'Functioning on one level, where I could walk and follow instructions, but that was it.'

One of his friends had given him a knife, which he had asked for. 'I don't know why I wanted a knife. I wanted protection or to hurt myself or still had visions of seeing the killers. I was irrational at the time. But anyway, one of Dad's mates at the airport took it off me.

'I still thought I was a suspect. I still thought I might have done it. That interview and my state of mind at the time had me thinking so unrealistically.'

As John's plane lifted off, his nearest and dearest returned to their cars and tried to pick up the pieces of their lives. It wasn't easy. The Cobby family had also been shattered by the murder. Pain was cascading through all of them, especially Gaynor. Having been so close to her sister-in-law, she was carrying deep grief and anguish. Several family members became fearful for themselves and consumed with anxiety about Gaynor, a young woman full of life and around the same age as Anita.

'My life changed so dramatically after her death,' Gaynor remembers. 'My family were worried all the time that something would happen to me. They reasoned that if it could happen to Anita, then anything was possible.

'We tried to get on with life, if you could call it that. I couldn't leave the house without having to reassure my family over and over that I would be okay. Mum and Gran would say, "Please make sure you are in a group. Keep your eyes open. Call me so I don't worry. Don't drink too much. Stay with your friends. Wait until they are inside the house before you drive off. Lock the car door, the front door. Check the windows . . ."'

Gaynor says that while the whole family had lost faith in the world, their greatest fear was for John. 'There was always this worry at the back of our minds that John would take his own life.

'My mother was a young woman of forty-nine when Anita died, and the grief she suffered, worrying about her only son and me, aged her dreadfully. The worry from that day onwards changed her lovely happy personality to one of constant worry and fear, which is with her to this day.'

Meanwhile, things in Michigan did not go as well as the Cobby family had hoped. John quickly spiralled into a pattern of self-abuse – drinking excessively, snorting cocaine and injecting heroin when he could.

'Totally out of control is the only way to describe it,' he

confesses, rolling his eyes in disbelief that he survived that period.

His friend Steven, despite being a qualified psychologist, realised he was unable to prevent John's slide from depression into an even more dangerous state of mind.

One night, Steven confessed to John that he had been keeping something back from him. He had delayed telling his friend because of John's fragile state of mind, but knew it had to be told sometime. The police had had a breakthrough in the investigation and criminal proceedings were under way.

Steven gave him scant information. John had made it clear that he had no desire to know what had happened to Anita – and he was in no state of mind to comprehend the details now.

'I knew there was an arrest of some kind but that's it. I had no details and didn't want to know.'

He was already on the verge of becoming a danger to himself with his reckless behaviour, but this news tipped him over the edge. Steven had John sign himself into the psychiatric ward at Pontiac Hospital in Michigan. There, while attempting to come to grips with his wife's death, John experienced one of the lowest points of his entire life.

'I was in this hospital surrounded by some really, really sick people. I shared this small room with another guy, called Michael. One morning, I was asleep on the bottom bunk when I felt this sticky stuff dripping onto my face. It was blood. Michael had somehow found a way to cut himself in the bunk above, had shredded himself with some razor blade and the blood was dripping on me. It was like a scene out of *One Flew Over the Cuckoo's Nest*. Surreal is the only way to describe it,' he says, closing his eyes as he tries to block out the memory.

Horrified, he checked himself out of the hospital immediately, not wanting to spend another minute in the madhouse. Somehow he convinced medical staff he was fine. In reality, he was anything but. He returned to Steven's home – back at square one. From there, the downhill slide continued, despite Steven's best efforts.

To keep body and soul together – or more accurately, to get enough money to buy drugs – he started working part-time as a dressing nurse in a local hospital, being paid cash under the table. 'I was using cocaine a lot and heroin when I could get it,' he tells me, shaking his head as he imitates putting a needle in his arm and pushing the syringe into his vein.

John also developed the habit of madly running for hours at a time, which stripped his weight down dramatically. 'It was snowing and I would just take off and run, run, run. It was totally contradictory. Here I was taking all these drugs and drinking madly but at the same time I was incredibly fit.'

Even in the driving snow and freezing conditions, whenever he hit the pavement Anita's image would be in his head. John Cobby was literally running away from his guilt over not having been there to protect her, running away from the fact he had nowhere to run to. There was nothing in his life or his future that he could see that was worth existing for. Except maybe in some parallel universe killing those who had taken Anita's life.

'I pushed myself that hard – I hoped I would just drop dead. I didn't die. I'm just a fucken coward,' he says repeatedly.

Throughout the hours of interviews I have had with John, there would not have been a single conversation when he didn't refer to himself as a coward. 'Gutless prick,' he would mutter, hating himself for being alive, for failing to protect Anita.

In a letter written to Anita's sister from America, its ink blurred by his tears, John wrote, 'Kathryn, I'm sorry that I have run away. I couldn't stay. I was very upset and unable to handle the situation. I hope you don't hate me for deserting you all. I'm sure I would have been a hindrance . . . Anita is my love and my only love. She is with me now and she will always be with me. I had a dream where I met her standing over a grave and went up to her and asked whose grave it was, and she said that it was hers, and although she is dead, she is always going to be with me. "I'm not really gone."'

One day, while he was still in Michigan, a journalist turned up on the doorstep of the house where he was staying, asking for John Cobby. It was only months after the murder. By then, some media organisations in Sydney were better informed and were extremely keen to interview Anita's mysterious husband. To date, though, no one had tracked him down.

'No one knew where I was except family and friends . . . all I know was it scared the shit out of me.' He doesn't know what news organisation they were from. No discussion took place with whoever it was, that was for sure.

For some reason, he assumed it was the *Daily Mirror*, my own paper, though to the best of my knowledge it wasn't. From among the scores of *Mirror* journalists who worked on the case, I never heard of anyone who found out John was in America or sent someone to knock on his door. At this stage, John and I were yet to meet.

Eventually, I did find out that quite a few racing journalists knew of the Cobby name and might have been able to figure out his whereabouts – who knows. None of them ever bothered to mention anything to the police reporters or news bosses. Years after the murder, I was told by a couple of racing guys that they hadn't wanted to upset anyone in the family and had assumed we mainstream journalists would find out anyway through our police contacts.

With John's boozing and drug-taking showing no signs of abating, and now with the possibility that the media had discovered where he was, his friends and family decided he should leave Michigan.

John's cousin Alan had a wealthy doctor friend named Dr Bob Hindi who lived in Albuquerque, New Mexico. A kindly soul, he owned an apartment in downtown San Francisco and offered it to John to come and go as he pleased. Everyone was hoping that the change of scenery would do John good, that it might break the cycle of depression and that somehow he would be able to get off the drugs.

'Bob Hindi was wonderful man and incredibly generous by giving me his apartment. But, really, nothing was working, and I just continued on my booze and drug trip, trying to obliterate everything. Not that it helped.'

He continued to party and run, completely unaware that back home, Sydney was now clamouring for the death penalty to be reintroduced ahead of the trial of Anita's killers. One night he drank an entire bottle of Southern Comfort before running to a bar called Ibeam, about 5 kilometres away from where he was staying, in the heart of San Francisco. 'I remember falling over, hurting my foot and getting up to keep running. I ended up in the bar, which was really famous at the time, and just danced all night on this sore foot. I had broken three bones in my right foot, I found out later, but didn't feel a thing at the time.'

Hours later, he snapped back into the here-and-now, finding himself in a strange house with a foot that was extremely painful. Totally wiped out, he rang a friend called Lisa who lived nearby. She collected him the next morning and took him to hospital. He then spent the next few weeks with Lisa in the small, well-to-do town of Woodside, near Stanford University.

'I remember being scared as hell and thinking, "I can't do this anymore." I hated drugs and the way I was living and was disappointed that I was still not able to kill myself.'

Realising he was penniless and completely out of control, and unnerved by the episode with his foot, he thought maybe going back home was the best option. Although he cannot remember how it was organised, next thing he knew he was going to Palo Alto and then to Los Angeles airport, and realised he was on his way back to Sydney.

He had no idea what to expect or do when he got home. That didn't worry him, but he was assuming – incorrectly, as he was about to discover – that all the publicity would have died down by now, that he wouldn't be constantly recognised, pointed at, questioned.

About an hour out of Sydney airport, John started to stir from the effects of the sleeping tablets and booze that he had taken to get on the plane. He slipped on the head phones and chose a music channel. Suddenly he found himself listening to the Simply Red song 'Holding Back the Years' and tears began to tumble down his face. It had been Anita's favourite song.

'I was sobbing and I didn't even realise it. A hostie came up to me and I blubbered something about going home and she gave me a bottle of champagne.'

It's possible that she figured out who he was. Cobby is an unusual surname. Maybe she felt sorry for him. John was always having thoughts like that.

Frankly, though, when he stepped off the plane he was almost unrecognisable. Over 1.8 metres in height, he weighed just 56 kilograms, he walked with a limp and his hair was falling out from a combination of stress and the abuse he had put his body through.

'It was heartbreaking to see him,' says Gaynor. 'It wasn't John. Not my handsome carefree brother with a cheeky grin that I grew up with.'

He never would be like that again.

CHAPTER 8

Catching the killers

February 1986

THE PRESSURE ON THE INVESTIGATORS to catch the killers remained at fever pitch. As well as coming from the police hierarchy, the government and the public, it came from the members of the task force themselves. The commitment of every individual working on the case bordered on the obsessive; it was hard not to be that way, especially for those who were dealing daily with the Lynch family.

The media were camped outside their home in O'Sullivan Street, a fact that worried investigators. Detective Ian Kennedy told Garry that if anyone stepped out of line or if it got too much for him, Garry should let him know and he would sort it out.

'The journalists were ringing or knocking on their door every day. Most of the time they were decent and respectful of the situation the family were in,' says Kennedy. '. . . I had to have a go at one journo for ringing them at some ungodly hour, but on the whole the media were pretty good.'

The Lynches would talk to the press nearly every morning,

never knocking back a request for an interview. They saw keeping Anita's murder in the public eye as their way of helping the police investigation. Garry told me later that he did twenty TV, radio and newspaper interviews while the investigation was in full swing. That's a big load for someone with no prior media experience; most politicians would only expect that kind of workload if there was an election coming up.

There was a strong media presence at Blacktown police station too. Teams of journalists were matching the police effort and working around the clock. The *Daily Mirror* had a car with a driver, reporter and photographer posted at the station twenty-four hours a day in case there was an arrest. So did the opposition newspaper, the Sydney *Sun*. Newspapers then produced four editions a day, and reporters were constantly updating the stories on Anita. TV crews were on standby as well.

All of that was fine by the task force. Like the Lynches, their strategy was to keep Anita's murder in the public eye. The constant hope was that public pressure would prompt someone to come forward with that vital piece of information, providing the breakthrough investigators were all sweating on. Consequently, detectives – especially Ian Kennedy – were feeding the media tidbits to keep them going.

Still, the police didn't share everything. Very early on, Detective Sergeant Graham Rosetta had been alerted to an individual by the name of John Travers, and told that he was an evil, twisted type who could well have done something like this. The man who contacted Rosetta said he had some information about Travers and a group of other men who might be connected to the crime.

'Travers had been involved in the rape of a man in Western Australia, where he held a knife to his throat while he raped him, and there was also a suggestion he was wanted for some attacks in South Australia,' Rosetta tells me.

Stories of an even more horrifying nature about Travers later came to light. 'We heard that on one occasion, he had sex with a sheep in his backyard and then slit its throat before cooking it and eating it. That gives you an idea of what type of person we were dealing with.'

Rosetta was born and bred in the country and came to Sydney as a young man to join the police force and also try his hand at rugby league, playing third grade for Balmain before an injury cut his career short. Like many cops of that era, he is a big man, and in those days cut an imposing figure. Unlike Ian Kennedy, he wasn't all that comfortable with the media back then and is still cautious about speaking to me. I am interested to find out more about the information he received from a local source that made the investigation look at Travers, which in turn led them to the rest of his gang.

'The person who came forward was very, very scared and feared for his life, as you would expect.' Even after so many years have passed, Rosetta won't give any details about his informant, believing there are still elements in the criminal community connected to the men in jail who could get him harmed.

When I raise the same topic with Speed Kennedy, he is just as vague and protective but reveals that the information about Travers and his accomplices arrived fairly early in the investigation.

'We were told they were at a party and disappeared for a long time, and when they came back they gave differing accounts of what they had been up to. It's the sort of thing that made us look at them pretty hard. And then the story about the sheep was impossible to ignore, considering how Anita was murdered.'

While the other investigators continued with the painstaking work of checking the alibis of known sex offenders and other possible suspects, a team of Blacktown detectives started to pursue the theory that Travers – as well as his longtime friend and fellow criminal Michael (Mick) Murdoch – could be who they were looking for.

Another name started to be bandied about too. Leslie Murphy's criminal record was unsavoury to say the least, fuelling the suspicion that he could also have been involved. Murphy was the youngest of nine children. Police were aware that he was not the only member of the family with a criminal record, although they focused solely on Les at this point, who was later discovered to be in a relationship with Travers's sister.

The turning point in the investigation came on 11 February, the day after Anita's funeral. Information was given to Detective Sergeant Rosetta that John Travers, Michael Murdoch and Leslie Murphy had stolen a car fitting the description of the one seen by the witness in Newton Road late on 2 February, and had been driving it around that night. Police were told the car had since been resprayed and its mag wheels replaced. No one else had come into the frame for the car theft or the murder at this stage.

'That became pivotal to our case and hunting down the gang,' says Kennedy.

Graham Rosetta tells me, 'By this time we were looking hard at Travers, Murdoch and [Les Murphy] as being the ones who killed Anita. We were sure it was linked to the stolen car.'

The effect of the breakthrough on the task force was electrifying. Now they at last had something concrete to chase. There was an air of excitement within the group that they might be closing in on the offenders.

As the hunt for the gang members began, everyone was sworn to secrecy. The last thing they wanted was for these guys to realise that the police were watching them. Though the three men were still young – Travers and Murdoch both eighteen, and Les Murphy twenty-two – they were all well-established crooks and rat-cunning into the bargain. If they got a whiff of

Nineteen and a genuine beauty. Anita Lorraine Lynch, crowned Miss Western Suburbs 1979, appearing alongside New South Wales Premier Neville Wran at a charity event.

A born nurse, with her caring nature and easy smile, Anita followed in her mother's footsteps. Graduation 1982.

The Cobby clan. Top (left to right): Kim, Gay, Julie, Pop Cobby, Greg, Sharan. Bottom (left to right): John in red skivvy, Karen, Mark, Nana, Louise.

The radiant couple with the priest who performed their marriage rites, 2 March 1982. Everything about the wedding, from the bride's dress to the backyard reception, was simple yet tasteful.

Anita and dog Lucy in 1981. Anita and
John loved sailing around Yowie Bay.

Life is good. A happily married man
with a beautiful wife, satisfying working
life and close-knit family.

The Cobbys at a friend's wedding in 1982 while living in Coffs Harbour, making the
most of their carefree lifestyle.

A total softie where dogs were concerned, Anita doted on Bessie (left) and Lucy (right).

The horse whisperer. Dealing with horses was intuitive for John, and training them was a dream he realised, with his wife's total support. John and Kermansha, Bowraville, 1982.

Photo courtesy John Cobby

Photo courtesy John Cobby

Photo courtesy John Cobby

Anita and John were one of those couples: effortlessly glamorous, yet never out to impress.

Globetrotters! Experiencing the delights of spring in Europe. After travelling the world, returning to daily life in Sydney was hard for Anita, but not for John. The decision to spend time apart was drama-free, and the two were in constant contact.

Off to work, late January 1986. Snapped by a professional, this lovely impromptu photo captured Anita's joy and optimism. After her murder five days later, the image cemented itself into the consciousness of a horrified Australia.

Does this jog anyone's memory? Constable Debbie Wallace re-enacts Anita's fateful train journey from Central Station to Blacktown. Although the strategy yielded little for investigators, it led to Wallace forming a lifelong bond with Anita's parents, Garry and Grace Lynch.

Co-leader of the investigation. For Detective Sergeant Ian 'Speed' Kennedy of Homicide Squad, there would be little sleep until whoever had killed Anita Cobby was found and brought to justice.

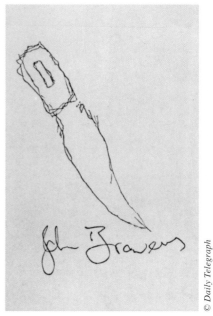

John Travers headed the list of suspects from early on in the investigation. His four accomplices gave conflicting accounts of the abduction and prolonged assault of Anita, but they were unanimous in naming him as the one who eventually finished her life.

When Detective Sergeant Graham Rosetta told Travers what investigators knew, and formally interviewed him, he asked Travers to draw the murder weapon. Travers did so with ease. His hands didn't tremble in the slightest as he produced this sketch.

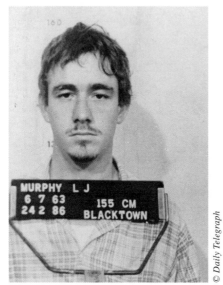

Caught in the act. In the early hours of 24 February 1986, police swooped on Les Murphy to arrest him for his part in the murder. They found the former sex worker in bed with two women.

Michael James 'Mick' Murdoch was a longtime friend of ringleader John Travers. Both men had extensive police records.

Aged eighteen when he participated in the Cobby murder, Mick Murdoch had been in and out of juvenile prisons throughout his childhood.

Don't mess with these guys. When officers went to arrest Gary Murphy, he burst out the door and headed for the fence, where he was intercepted by members of the Special Weapons and Operations Section.

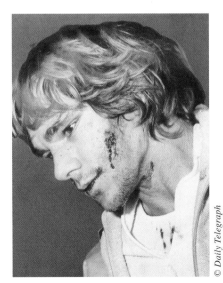

No one denied that the SWOS officers had pushed Murphy's head into the wooden fence. Murphy's barrister, Leigh Johnson, argued that her client's confession – made within hours of his arrest – was given under extreme duress.

Older but not wiser. Michael Patrick Murphy, aged thirty-three at the time of the murder, was a father.

Gotcha. Michael Murphy had a string of convictions to his name, including for armed hold-up. Journalists digging into his past discovered that he had busted out of jail: Murphy was an escaped prisoner on the run.

Detective Ian Kennedy (far left) escorts Michael Murphy to the Boiler Paddock, where farmer John Reed discovered Anita's body.

© Daily Telegraph

A nation reels. The public outpouring of grief spilled over into anger when the five men were formally charged with the murder of Anita Lorraine Cobby.

© Daily Telegraph

Capital punishment was abolished in New South Wales in 1955. Many members of the public went out of their way to urge for it to be reinstated – for the Cobby killers. Security around the prisoners was tightened during all court appearances.

Newly minted barrister Leigh Johnson, who represented Gary Murphy, received a lot of negative attention in the press. Johnson was simply doing her job – even the most hardened criminal has the right to a fair trial.

June 1987. Anita's parents, Garry and Grace Lynch, are surrounded by media representatives as they reflect on the historic verdict handed down by Justice Alan Maxwell. The reporter in the background holding the notepad is author Mark Morri.

Poles apart. While the Lynches were fronting the media, always dignified, brave and polite, John Cobby was grieving Anita's death with denial, drugs and drink.

Ian 'Speed' Kennedy was among the mourners after Garry Lynch passed away in 2008. Here the retired detective is being greeted by Garry's widow, Grace. She was a person who always lived up to her name.

ANITA
ANITA LORRAINE COBBY
1959 – 1986

"HER LIGHT SHINES FOREVER"

Following the funeral service for his former mother-in-law, Grace 'Peg' Lynch, John Cobby visited Anita's gravesite – for only the second time in twenty-seven years. His first visit was at the suggestion of a psychologist who could see that John was struggling to accept Anita's death.

Café regulars. Author Mark Morri and John Cobby have known each other for nearly thirty years. Thanks to a chance meeting at Bronte Beach, what started out as a journalist's pursuit of a story turned into a genuine friendship based on trust.

Surfing has been a constant source of solace in John Cobby's life. Even in the worst depths of pain and confusion – and the guilt that dogs him to this day – hitting the waves always lifts his spirits.

the police interest in them, they would disappear. And they had a network of fellow criminals who would help them.

It was a reasonable assumption that the killers would be jumpy and secretive in their movements anyway. They would have observed the public fury at their act and known to keep their heads down. At the best of times, the three had a transient lifestyle that consisted of wandering from place to place, often getting drunk and stoned and crashing wherever they could. Plus they drifted in and out of contact with each other. These were not everyday citizens who kept regular hours or lived a routine life. They squatted at people's homes and spent their days drinking in pubs or smoking pot often financed from petty crimes such as burglary and bag snatches.

The information police had, though powerful, was scant, and they had to go back to basics in their search for the men. For the next week, they enlisted the help of a number of informants to gather intelligence on Travers, Murdoch and Les Murphy. Investigators scoured the western suburbs for traces of the suspects, discreetly checking out all the local pubs for starters. They followed up every possible sighting of one or more of the three men.

Rosetta asked his source if he could give him anything to help police locate Travers in particular. From the start, Travers was their number-one target. Once they had the address of his family home – given to them by informants – investigators covertly staked it out, but with no luck.

'They were long, long days,' recalls Kennedy. 'Everyone was working their guts out all hours of the day and night but no one was complaining. Everyone was driven by their own motivation to catch these guys.'

The net around the fugitives was slowly tightening.

Friday 21 February 1986

Anticipation was running high. Police now had the names of three people who might have been involved in the murder or the theft of the car. They also had reasonable intelligence as to the whereabouts of Travers and Murdoch, believed to be staying in the same house, and of Les Murphy. It was time to bring the three in for questioning – and hopefully get them to incriminate themselves or, by some miracle, confess to the murder.

In 1986 it was a lot easier to bring someone in for questioning than it is today. Police didn't need warrants. Besides, all three had criminal records and Travers was already wanted on warrants for rape in Western Australia and also in the Sydney suburb of Toongabbie. They were supposedly being brought in to assist police with their inquiries, rather than being arrested. Although nothing had been leaked to the media, police were sure all the suspects would be on edge, ready to run at a moment's notice.

At six o'clock on the Friday morning the detectives on the case met in the operation room of Blacktown police station and broke into two groups, one led by Graham Rosetta and the other, consisting of Homicide Squad detectives, by Speed Kennedy. Each was handed the address of the location they were going to raid. Members of the Tactical Response Group (TRG) were attached to both groups. A heavily armed and highly trained unit, the TRG specialised in going into hostile environments and were authorised to use high-powered weapons. During high-risk arrests, they were always first in the door, usually thanks to the use of a massive sledgehammer. They were not known for their subtlety and were often called the Terribly Rough Guys.

As the teams assembled at Blacktown police station, Speed Kennedy – himself a former TRG member and a qualified police negotiator – addressed everyone who would be involved in the two raids. He warned them against getting carried away with the emotion and adrenaline he was sure were pumping through their veins.

A short time later, Graham Rosetta and his team prepared to storm the home of John Travers's uncle in Wentworthville. The uncle and his girlfriend were particularly close to Travers, and he often overnighted at their place. Travers referred to his uncle's girlfriend as his aunty, even though the pair were not married. She was to become a central figure in the case against the killers.

Rosetta and two fellow detectives slipped around the side of the house, first kicking in a gate to gain access to the property. His colleagues rushed ahead of him, and Rosetta has a vivid memory of hearing an almighty crash from inside the house.

'The guys had somehow broken a large fish tank in the loungeroom and there was water and tropical fish all over the floor. About a year later, the woman who owned the home sent a bill to the police department for a new fish tank.' With a wry smile, he adds, 'I don't know if it was paid.'

As the fish lay flailing on the carpet, Travers and Murdoch were dragged out of the bed they happened to be sharing and were promptly taken into custody, to be questioned primarily over the theft of the motor vehicle. It has never been established whether the two were sexual partners, but it was well known that Travers wasn't choosy about the gender of those he had sex with.

A search of the residence was conducted. Under the bed where Travers and Murdoch had been sleeping, officers found a bloodstained knife in a sheath and took it into evidence. Could it be the murder weapon? Rosetta was certainly hoping it was.

Meanwhile, the team led by Ian Kennedy had taken Les Murphy into custody. They arrested him at John Travers's family home, where they also took possession of a Holden station wagon that had a set of mag wheels.

The three were taken back to Blacktown police station and interviewed. These interviews were predominantly focused on the theft of the motor vehicle, and while police asked each of the three about the murder of Anita they all denied any involvement. Police were sure they were guilty but didn't have enough to charge them with the murder.

'Before we got them in custody, we had our strategy worked out,' Kennedy says. 'We would talk to them about the car, telling them we thought it was the vehicle involved in the murder, and gauge their reactions. And also try and lock them into saying where they were and what they were doing at the time. Their body language clearly satisfied us that they were involved in the murder but we needed proof. We were close but not quite there.'

Maybe it was out of arrogance or maybe it was bravado but none of the three asked for lawyers.

For two hours, Detective Sergeant Rosetta questioned Travers about the stolen car and the knife retrieved from under the bed. What were Rosetta's impressions of the man?

'He was cold. The coldest person I have ever encountered. When I asked him about the knife, he just looked at me and said, "I didn't slit that slut's throat."'

Rosetta shakes his head slightly, still not able to believe a human being could be so detached while discussing delivering a fatal wound.

Rosetta emphasises that at that point he hadn't mentioned anything about Anita's murder. All he had told Travers was that he wanted to know how the blood got on the knife. Travers maintained that the blood belonged to a sheep he had killed a month or so ago in his backyard.

Like all the detectives on the case, Rosetta had heard about Travers's experience with the sheep. Without giving away that he was aware of that story, Rosetta quizzed Travers about how and why he had killed the sheep. With a slight shrug, Travers answered, 'You gotta eat. I cut its throat.'

Never in his life had Rosetta felt such disgust towards anyone. Here, sitting in front of him, was someone – a so-called human being – who could engage in sex with an animal, then casually slaughter and eat it. During the hour-long interview Rosetta remembers that Travers kept pricking his finger with a paper clip, drawing blood, then licking it off.

Meanwhile, Murdoch was taken by police to the address from which the car had been stolen and gave them a statement saying he had been involved. Again he denied having had anything to do with the killing of Anita Cobby.

Next, all three were formally charged with motor vehicle theft. But police handled Travers differently from the other two. He was kept in custody because he was a suspect in connection with the rapes in the Toongabbie area as well as the rape in Western Australia. He voluntarily provided a blood sample in relation to those investigations.

Police made sure Murdoch and Murphy were granted conditional bail at the cop shop – without having to appear in court. Some 'dogs' – police jargon for a surveillance team – were ready and waiting for them when they walked out of the station. From the minute they were released, the pair were tailed by these specialised police, highly trained in following criminals. Their every move would be monitored and reported back to Kennedy and his colleagues.

Increasingly convinced the pair had been involved in the Cobby murder, police were not going to let them out of their sight. There was also the possibility that they would lead police to other suspects not yet identified. It was probably too much to hope that Murdoch and Murphy might try to find the missing car and get rid of any incriminating evidence left after the murder, but there was always a chance they might slip up. Things were moving quickly.

Then out of the blue Travers sent word to the police station sergeant that he wanted to talk to his 'aunty' – his uncle's partner – and could she visit him and bring some smokes. At the time police didn't think anything of the request, but it paved the way for something that would prove pivotal in the case.

It was about 5 pm when the station sergeant rang the woman then handed the phone to Detective Sergeant Kevin Raue. He spoke slowly as he explained that John had been arrested on motor theft charges and had asked if she would bring him some cigarettes. He had no idea who the woman was or where the conversation would lead.

'The minute she got on the phone, she began to cry and was highly emotional as she began talking,' reveals Raue, now an advisor to the Solomon Islands Government's corrective services and justice departments.

'I need to talk to you. I need to talk about John. It's about his behaviour towards women,' Raue recalls her saying. 'Then she told me she was on the verge of ringing police herself and wanted to meet with me.'

For the previous two weeks, she had been having trouble sleeping, burdened by information about Travers that she felt police should know. She had been frightened about the consequences that such actions would unleash, but now, with the police calling her, she decided to grab the chance to clear her conscience.

The conversation was fairly brief. The pair arranged to meet in an hour's time at Wentworthville Leagues Club, just 10 kilometres away from the station. The woman told Raue she would be wearing a blue dress.

As he put the receiver down, Raue frowned to himself. There had already been numerous false leads in the investigation, as is true of many cases, yet this somehow felt a little different. The woman sounded genuine, and Travers had reached out to her. Obviously the teenage murder suspect sitting in the cells below the detectives' office trusted her.

The woman, who was soon to become the star witness in

the murder case and would be codenamed Miss X, arrived at the popular Western Suburbs Leagues Club promptly at six o'clock. Detectives Rosetta and Heskett went inside the club, while Raue waited outside on the steps. 'I saw a woman in a light blue dress hovering around looking nervous,' Raue recalls. 'I went up to her, introduced myself and asked if she was the woman I had spoken to earlier, and she just nodded.'

Even before she spoke, Raue could tell the woman was petrified. He reached out and gently touched her on the arm; he couldn't help but notice that it bore the telltale signs of a former heroin addiction. Next he led her to a darkened section of the car park, where they got into his vehicle – an unmarked police car.

Blanketed in the security of the police car and shielded by darkness, Miss X poured out the troubling things she knew about John Travers. Basically, she had a strong belief that John had been involved in the murder of Anita Cobby. Travers had told her about previous acts of violence he had committed – for instance, he had raped both men and women when he was interstate. He liked knives, she added, and had one with him wherever he went.

Her instincts told her Travers had participated in the murder, but she had no evidence.

The conversation ended with Raue saying he would be in touch. She quietly got out of the car, was swallowed up by the darkness and made her way home.

Impressed by the woman's insights into Travers, Raue went back inside the club, where his fellow detectives were still waiting, and told them he thought they were onto something. Together they headed back to the station.

As the senior member of the Homicide Squad, Ian Kennedy was called in from home: Travers would be expecting Miss X to visit him the next day, so there was no time to waste. How were they to respond to this latest development?

Putting their heads together, the four detectives hatched a plan. The best course of action, they concluded, was to get Miss X to come into Blacktown police station in the morning, give Travers the cigarettes that he had requested and see what happened. If the woman could get Travers talking, chances were he would spell out what he had done to Anita Cobby and the police would be sure of all their assumptions.

Saturday 22 February

As Saturday morning shoppers started going about their business in the heart of Blacktown, Raue, Heskett and Rosetta were already hard at work in an upper level of the station. A tired old building, it was the nerve centre of the hunt for Anita's killer or killers, and there were signs all through the office of the intense investigation. Desks were covered with paperwork, there were ties and suit jackets draped over chairs, and half-filled coffee cups were scattered everywhere.

Raue picked up the phone, rang Miss X and asked her to come into the station and pay a visit to her 'nephew'.

It was mid-morning when the woman arrived. She was immediately taken up to the detectives' office, where she was greeted by Raue. He sat her down and made her a cup of coffee to help settle her nerves. They discussed the fact that police believed a stolen car had been involved in the murder and that perhaps Travers would talk about it to her.

'We didn't give her a script of any set questions. All we asked was that she go and talk to him and listen.'

The custody manager was told to inform Travers that his aunt had arrived with some cigarettes. As was routine, police had taken everything from him, including his tobacco, before putting him into a cell.

Raue accompanied Miss X down to the cells, reassuring her that she was doing the right thing and that they wouldn't let anything bad happen to her. Raue stopped a few metres short of the small cell holding Travers and a young uniformed officer escorted her the rest of the way. They knew that if the suspect spotted a detective, he would smell a rat. Raue positioned himself out of sight behind a counter, but in a spot where he could observe the woman through some glass panelling.

There was a small opening in the cell through which food was passed to prisoners, and Miss X walked up to it, greeted Travers and gave him his smokes. For the next twenty minutes, they faced each other and spoke through this opening. The woman's legs appeared to be shaking uncontrollably the whole time, and Raue feared that Travers would notice how on edge she was and suspect that something was wrong. Fortunately this did not happen, and eventually Raue could tell from her body language that Miss X was saying goodbye.

It looked as though she was holding her breath as she walked the 20 metres to where Raue was waiting. Quickly he ushered her out a side door into a courtyard near the police car park. Recalls Raue, 'She collapsed into my arms crying and said, "He did it. He killed her."'

The next step was to put in writing what had just taken place. Miss X was guided back up to the detectives' office, and they showed her to a chair in front of a desk. Raue seated himself behind the desk, inserted a sheet of paper into an ancient Remington typewriter, and began to type out her statement. Slightly calmer now, she repeated for Raue in as much detail as possible what Travers had told her.

'They are trying to pin the murder on me,' Travers had said to her almost immediately.

Then, despite her trembling legs, she got right to the heart of the matter. 'I held his hand, put it against my face and said, "Did you do it, John?" And I started crying.'

It seemed that now he was in custody, Travers wanted some favours from Miss X. He wanted her to take care of evidence that connected him with the murder.

'Go home [to the house of Travers's mother] and get the knife with a brown wooden handle out of the knife drawer,' he said, without telling her what to do with it. She hadn't been sure whether she was supposed to get rid of it; maybe Travers wanted her to hide it somewhere so he could keep it as a trophy. Rather than pursue that line of questioning, however, she had asked Travers if that was the knife he'd used to kill Anita. He had replied, 'Yeah. It's my best knife.'

And as if that were no big deal, he had quickly moved on to other instructions: 'Get the jeans; they are really faded.' He'd known they had Anita's blood on them. Again, he hadn't elaborated on what Miss X was to do with the evidence. She'd had the impression that his mind was racing as he tried to think through what else could tie him to the murder.

Travers had then told her to go and see Les Murphy and tell him to make sure he got rid of the car, because 'the police know all about it'.

With those instructions out of the way, Travers had spoken freely about the events of Sunday 2 February. How they had all been in on it – he, Michael Murdoch, Les Murphy and his brothers Michael and Gary had all had sex with Anita. During the retelling he had seemed proud of himself, and at one stage Miss X had asked him to stop laughing as he described the repeated rape of Anita Cobby.

'They were saying, "Trawney [Travers's nickname], do your thing",' he told Miss X, referring to how – as his mates all knew – he'd enjoyed taking a sheep and cutting its throat.

For Miss X, it had been a relief when the visit came to an

end. She finished her statement by describing how she had bidden her partner's murderous nephew goodbye and been escorted from the cells.

As Raue tapped out the last few words, she flopped back in her chair, utterly drained by the ordeal.

While Travers had admitted to Miss X that he had killed Anita, his confession was uncorroborated and would not stand up in court. In legal terms, it was hearsay. Travers could deny having said it. Also, a good defence lawyer would tear strips off the woman in the witness box. For starters, she was a self-confessed former drug addict with a police record. Demolishing her credibility as a witness would be a piece of cake. The police needed hard evidence to make the case watertight before charging Travers with murder.

If Miss X had needed guts to visit Travers in the cells, now came serious pressure. Police asked her if she would pay Travers a second visit, this time with a tape recorder concealed under her clothing. Could she see if she could get him to confess again? Everything was moving fast for Miss X, but she took a deep breath and nodded.

In agreeing to this, she was taking a significant personal risk. A huge chunk of her social network had just been potentially sacrificed. How would her partner react? Would he stick by her or see this as a betrayal of his family? Leaving aside the morality of the situation, how would the Travers family react when they realised – as they would sooner or later – that she had played this part in bringing John in? But former junky or not, she knew the difference between right and wrong, and she realised she could never 'unhear' his casual admission of an act of pure evil. Would John Travers ever be able to control his urges? He had expressed no regret. Who would his next victim be? And the one after that?

While Miss X sat alone with her thoughts, Raue telephoned Kennedy at home and relayed the details of her cell visit. The call was short and to the point. Kennedy agreed that while it was gold, they had to have more than the woman's word.

As soon as he got off the phone, Raue flicked through the pages of the freshly typed up and sworn statement from Miss X, drew up a warrant authorising the surveillance and raced it across to the legal department. The next step was to have the warrant rubber-stamped by a judge.

It must have been a long wait for Miss X while the detectives were attending to the legalities of the wire. Sitting there, cut off from all contact with her partner and two children, did she have second thoughts? Consider changing her mind?

Next, as another sign of how serious it all was, police went and collected her family and brought them to her at the station. When her partner – John Travers's uncle – was apprised of the situation, he immediately agreed to support her. It was dangerous and brave but the right thing to do. And it sealed everything for the equally brave Miss X. The two children – Miss X's daughter from another relationship and the couple's 5-year-old son – were taken to a friend's place.

The uncle and Miss X now agreed to visit Les Murphy's house and deliver Travers's message about abandoning the car. The hope was that he would panic and head straight to the vehicle while the surveillance team discreetly followed.

Things didn't end up going to plan. In fact, police never did find the stolen Holden used to abduct Anita.

By the time the pair arrived back at the station, the place was buzzing. The warrant to use a listening device had been signed by Justice Slattery. Police now had the green light to execute their plan.

The technical support team was called in so they could work out the best way to wire up Miss X. If the taping session worked, the recording would be the nail in the coffin for Travers and his associates. If all went well, Kennedy and his colleagues would soon catch the Cobby killers.

In 1986, this kind of surveillance equipment was still fairly crude. A reel-to-reel recording device had to be wrapped around the woman's stomach, and its wires sticky-taped to a microphone on her chest. She was wearing jeans and a sloppy Joe, and she prayed there would be no telltale lumps protruding from her top, no wires showing. It was nerve-racking.

'We were worried it might not pick up their conversation, but it was the best we had at the time,' says Rosetta.

Finally, everything had been tested and the tech boffins gave the thumbs-up. Raue guided Miss X back to the cells. Raue gave her a reassuring nod as he went back to the same spot where he had watched her during her first visit.

Her stomach churning, but knowing she was doing the right thing, the woman was psyching herself up with every step. Most of all, she was willing herself to speak to Travers in a normal voice. If anything about her appearance or behaviour aroused his suspicion, the whole thing would be a disaster. The listening device was biting into her skin, and her entire body was trembling with fear.

Hoping against hope that the self-confessed murderer would not notice how very scared she was, Miss X approached Travers's cell, clutching some cigarettes. When they had spoken that morning, she had promised to bring him some more. Now it was early evening. Hopefully he would assume that the cops had let her back in so she could give them to him, and he wouldn't get suspicious.

But Travers seemed to be so wrapped up in himself that he took in nothing about her appearance. He didn't pause to wonder why she had been allowed back in to see him so soon after her previous visit earlier that day. Instead, getting straight to business, he quizzed her about practical matters, asking whether she had got rid of his jeans and knife.

She told him she had done as he had said and got rid of the clothes but had been unable to find the knife. 'What do you think happened to that knife?' she asked. Perhaps Les had got rid of it or maybe Travers had hidden it somewhere himself.

'No, it's me best knife,' he responded, then added, 'I want to keep it if you find it.'

As during the previous conversation, once they'd gone through Travers's requirements for dealing with possessions that could become evidence against him, he had no difficulty in discussing the murder in detail.

Over the previous few hours, the fact that police had taken a sample of blood from him had been playing on his mind. The streetwise Travers knew he was in deep trouble and could see only one way out: escape. Blacktown police station was right near the railway station and he had come up with a daring plan involving Gary Murphy and Michael Murdoch:

'Get them to derail a train. Send it through the fucken walls. And get Mick and Gary to get me out . . . I have an oxy [welding torch] at home.'

Realising as he said it how ridiculous it sounded, Travers cancelled that instruction and came up with a more old-fashioned plan:

'Tell Gary and Mick to be at the back of the police station here [he pointed in the direction he was referring to], with a couple of shotties [shotguns] between 3 and 3.30 in the morning before I go to court. It's only a skeleton crew at that time. The oldest bloke has got the keys. They don't check on me, when the sun comes up; [just] during the night about four times.'

The shotties were needed, he said, 'to bust me out'.

Laugh? Cry? Throw up? All of them seemed like good options as Miss X walked back down the corridor to where Raue had been pacing, waiting for her. Minutes later, police had removed the listening device and pushed a glass of water in front of her as she collected her thoughts. God, she needed a ciggie.

She could hardly believe she'd done it. It was a miracle he had not noticed the bulkiness of her clothing.

The detectives spoke, breaking into her thoughts. They were smiling, nodding, thanking her. For God's sake, she deserved a bloody Oscar for that performance.

She closed her eyes. Her heart was pounding but there was a lightness around her jaw, neck and shoulders. Whatever happened, at least she could live with her conscience.

Sunday 23 February

Police now had hard evidence that Michael Murdoch and Les Murphy were implicated with Travers in Anita's murder. But they had two more names to add to their list of alleged killers: Les Murphy's older brothers Gary (twenty-eight) and Michael (thirty-three).

Police knew exactly where to find Les Murphy and Michael Murdoch because surveillance teams had been shadowing their every move since they had been released from Blacktown police station on Friday afternoon. It was decided to arrest the pair under the cover of darkness on the Sunday night.

Police wired up Miss X again and asked her to pay Murdoch a visit, to see if she could get more information from him and maybe learn the whereabouts of the two other Murphy brothers.

By now she was becoming more at ease with wearing a wire, but the conversation didn't yield much. When she spoke to a cautious Michael Murdoch on the front lawn he told her very little, other than that he was thinking of heading interstate.

Afterwards, Miss X walked quietly down the street, where she was met by police who had stealthily positioned themselves nearby. No doubt she was mightily relieved as the listening device was removed from her for what would be the last time.

From that day on, however, Miss X's life – like the lives of all those closely associated with the murder of Anita Cobby – would be forever changed. After she was whisked away, she and her family were placed into the witness protection program and given new identities.

'We couldn't get near her [after that] without going through the program,' says Kevin Raue. 'Even as the trial approached and we would want to go over evidence it was strictly by the book and we had no idea where she was.'

As midnight approached, teams of heavily armed police were deployed to various locations around the western suburbs. On the strength of Miss X's visit to Murdoch earlier in the day, they had hoped to arrest all four of the alleged killers, but instead they only managed to get two of them.

Murdoch was arrested at his mother's home, where he was staying. Les Murphy was found hiding in a bed with two women at a house in Granville. Neither put up a fight when police pointed their weapons at them.

Next police went to Travers's home in Doonside, where they executed a search warrant that had been drawn up and signed that day, after Travers had spilled his guts to his aunt. They tore the place apart and located the clothes Travers had been wearing on the night he murdered Anita, the ones he had asked Miss X to destroy. They also found a number of knives, which were sent for testing.

Meanwhile Graham Rosetta prepared to spend the next few hours talking to the most evil man he would ever deal with.

*

It was shortly before 4.40 am and John Raymond Travers was sleeping when Rosetta and another detective, Paul Rynne, walked down from their office to the cells. By then, Murphy and Murdoch had been interviewed and named Travers as the person solely responsible for Anita's death.

Rosetta roused Travers from his slumber, confronting him even as he was rising from the bed with the fact that police had new information about the Anita Cobby murder that pointed to Travers.

There was no denial from the now-alert Travers, who looked at the detective with his dead eyes and asked, 'Who gave us up?'

He was brought up from his cell and put in an interview room to be questioned by detectives Rosetta and Rynne.

'He was matter of fact and showed no emotion,' Rosetta recalls.

Then out it came: the story of brutal depravity around the last few hours of the life of Anita Lorraine Cobby. How Travers and Murdoch had grabbed her as she walked along Newton Road, forcing her into their stolen car. How they had immediately yanked her clothes off and raped her in the car. How they had rifled through her purse and used the money to buy petrol at a service station, holding her down all the while so no one observed her. How they had then driven out to Reen Road, where all five took turns raping her in a manner that is indescribable.

Although sickened by what he was hearing, Rosetta pressed on with his questioning, getting Travers to take him through the night, step by step. This is how the conversation went when Rosetta asked Travers about the knife he had used to kill Anita:

Rosetta: Was it in a sheath?

Travers: Yes.

Rosetta: Where is it now?

Travers: It should be at my mother's.

Rosetta: Do you remember whereabouts at your mother's?

Travers: It should be in the kitchen drawer.

Rosetta: Will you tell us how you cut her throat?

Travers: Just pulled back her head and cut her throat.

Rosetta: Do you recall how many times you cut her throat?

Travers: No, I just pulled her head back and I think I sliced it twice.

Rosetta: What degree of force did you use when you cut her throat?

Travers: I pressed a fair bit. The knife's pretty sharp.

Rosetta: At what side of the body were you standing when you cut the throat?

Travers: I was standing with my legs spread over the top of her.

Rosetta: Were you in a crouched or upright position?

Travers: Crouched.

Rosetta: In what hand did you hold the knife?

Travers: Right hand.

Rosetta: Were you doing anything with your left hand?

Travers: I was holding her head back.

Rosetta: How were you holding her head?

Travers: By her hair.

Rosetta: Was Mrs Cobby conscious at the time you cut her throat?

Travers: No.

Rosetta: Do you recall seeing any blood?

Travers: Yeah.

Rosetta: Where was the blood?

Travers: Over me hands, all on the knife. It sort of sprayed on me feet and jeans.

Finally, there it was: the full confession of the murder of Anita Cobby, signed by John Travers.

Disturbingly, during the three hours and fifteen minutes in which John Travers was interrogated, he never once showed any emotion or remorse about what he had done. At one point, at Rosetta's request, he calmly drew a picture of the type of knife he had used to kill Anita; his hands didn't shake, not even for a second.

The opportunity for the detectives to reflect would come later, however. For the moment, the investigation was approaching a climax.

Monday 24 February

It was 5.30 in the morning. Detective Sergeant Ian Kennedy had just broken the news of the arrests to the head of the Homicide Squad, Ken Webster, who had phoned the boss of the Criminal Investigation Bureau, who had rung the Police Commissioner, John Avery.

Now he had a promise to keep.

He knocked on the door of the Lynch home, summoning the father of Anita Cobby from his bed. He had vital news, and he did not want Grace and Garry to hear it on the radio.

'We got three of them, Garry, but there's another two,' Kennedy announced after the door swung open. Then he went inside to explain the events of the last twenty-four hours and to share what investigators had learned.

'It was a difficult thing to tell him, that there were more than three attackers involved. I knew it would play on his mind.' Yet Kennedy was – and still is – a man of his word, and he had promised Garry Lynch that he would tell him the minute something broke on the case.

'I also wanted him to know that it was a reward, in a way, for the effort he and Grace had gone through fronting the media every day.'

The fact that five individuals had been involved in his daughter's murder did hit Garry hard. The big detective watched the man as he grappled with that information; the unbidden thoughts that popped into his head about the things Anita must have endured.

By contrast, for John Cobby, piecing together the full picture would be an agonisingly slow process. In his current fragile state, the last thing he could deal with was a reminder of Anita's suffering and death. For years, he knew only the basics: that several men had been responsible. For a long time, that was about as much information as he could cope with.

*

It was now nearing nine o'clock on Monday morning. The cops had been going flat out since Travers had asked to see his 'aunty' on Friday afternoon. By now, the statements of all three accused had been typed up and put in individually labelled manila folders, ready to be given to police prosecutors.

Everyone connected with the case – police, journalists and the public – remembers the events that unfolded as word spread that the Cobby killers had been caught. The day 24 February 1986 became one of the most dramatic days ever seen in Sydney. You often hear the expression 'The crowd went wild', and the word 'wild' perfectly describes the mood that day.

In New South Wales, individuals accused of serious crimes make a formal appearance in the court of trial to hear the charges against them, in the presence of a judge. This is when they enter a plea of guilty or not guilty. The day the three men were driven to court, a mob gathered outside Blacktown police station baying for blood. Placards bearing the words 'Hang the bastards' were being worn by mothers and even grandmothers as they waited to set eyes on the men accused of the murder. Workmen fashioned pieces of rope into nooses and hung them over the sides of buildings opposite the police station.

'It was unbelievable, and something I have never seen in Australia before or since,' says Kennedy today. 'The crowd were rocking the police car, trying to get to them. We were driving through them slowly, with the mob completely surrounding the car.'

The bystanders were full of hate and many had worked themselves into a frenzy. Scores of police were deployed around the station and the adjacent courthouse throughout the rest of the day.

While the crowds outside vented their outrage, the three accused made their appearance in court. The *Daily Mirror* had stationed journalists inside, and I was outside among the ever-increasing number of people.

The court appearance was almost an anticlimax. In less than five minutes, the charges of car theft, and the assault, rape and murder of Anita Cobby were read out by the police prosecutor, Bruce Newling. None of the accused muttered a word.

But the job wasn't done yet. Michael and Gary Murphy were still at large. All the efforts of Kennedy and his men were now focused on finding and apprehending them.

As police pursued the brothers, there were false sightings all over western Sydney and, in fact, Australia. Acting on tip-offs from the public, as well as from informants who were being leaned on, police raided several homes – but to no avail.

After four days of intense activity, a phone call was received from a reliable source alerting police that the Murphys were holed up in a townhouse in Tar Place, Glenfield. By ten o'clock that night, more than fifty heavily armed police were positioned around the perimeter of the property, ready to intercept anyone who bolted from the premises, and two teams were preparing to enter the house.

Once again, before the teams had left on the raid, Kennedy had reminded them to be professional, to keep hold of their emotions and simply to carry out the job at hand. 'Bring these men to justice for the family,' he urged, and warned them not jeopardise the case in any way. It was advice he was also giving to himself.

The police helicopter hovering nearby flew over the block of units and turned on its powerful searchlight. A TRG officer smashed in the door, then Kennedy, Raue and Rosetta entered. They found Michael Murphy sitting in the loungeroom with a woman, Debra McAskill, and a small child. (McAskill was later charged with harbouring a fugitive and jailed.) Gary Murphy, who was also in the loungeroom, decided to make a break for it, and dashed from the house into the backyard.

Kennedy pointed his shotgun at Michael Murphy and ordered him to lie on the ground. Kennedy planted his size eleven and a half foot on Murphy's head as he kept the shotgun trained on Murphy's temple.

'Murphy was a hardened criminal, convicted of a number of armed hold-ups, and an escapee. He was dangerous and I wasn't going to take any chances,' Kennedy comments.

With his finger on the trigger of the shotgun and the adrenaline pumping, you can only wonder at what was going through Kennedy's mind. In that instant, did he picture the scene in that paddock, the eyes of that young woman staring hauntingly in death?

Kennedy won't say if he had to steel himself not to pull the trigger, admitting only: 'There was a woman and child in the room. I had a job to do and that was to arrest these guys for the murder of Anita. And nothing else.'

Outside, Gary Murphy almost made it to the back fence before he too was taken into custody. In the process, his head was pushed into the wooden paling, leaving him marked and bloodied. He also wet himself, and the photos in the next day's paper clearly showed his stained pants.

One police officer said with glee, 'They will like seeing that inside. The other prisoners will see him as the coward he is and it won't be pretty for him.'

On the drive back to the station, Michael Murphy began to spill his guts, basically saying that although he had been present, it had been the others who had had sex with Anita, not him. Travers had been the one who'd killed her, without any prompting from his associates. Like all the others except for Travers, he was only too willing to give up his so-called mates, and at the same time distance himself from the actual rape and murder.

Back at the station, Kennedy began the interview of Michael Murphy. The sickening details that emerged completely matched what John Travers had told Graham Rosetta, except that Murphy downplayed his own part in the events.

Kennedy: Do you agree that en route to this police station I asked you to tell me your story about the incident with Anita Cobby?

Michael Murphy: Yes.

Kennedy: I will now ask you to reiterate what you said about this incident, commencing from early in the evening, when you joined up with the other people you nominated.

Michael Murphy: We were all at the Doonside Hotel. We were there for a couple of hours drinking. John [Travers] decided that he wanted to go to Windsor.

Murphy said they all drove to a house in Windsor, where Travers went inside for a few minutes, and it was on the drive back that they spotted Anita Cobby walking down the street.

'He seen that Anita walking down the street. I was driving. He said, "Go turn around. I'll grab her." And he said to Mick [Murdoch], "You are going to help me." Mick said, "Yes."

'We drove past her and pulled up as she walked past. John jumped out of the car and grabbed her and started dragging her in. He said to Mick, "Help." Mick jumped out of the car and helped drag her in.

'I drove off . . . um, the door was still open . . . um, John said to her, "Shut up and you won't get hurt."

'She said, "Why are you doing this? I'm married." Again John told her to shut up.'

Kennedy: What happened then?

Michael Murphy: He started giving directions and I didn't know where to go, so I told Gary to drive. Um, the car was still going, and we swapped places as the car was going. We came to this

112

kinda hill. The car stalled. I think we were going to run out of
petrol . . . um, we started the car again . . . um, John and Mick
pushed the girl onto the floor and told her to be quiet.

Murphy then described how they rifled through Anita's purse.
They used $15 of her money to buy some petrol. They then
continued towards Prospect, with Travers giving directions to
Reen Road, where they parked.

'Les said, "There's a car parked down in front." So Mick
said, "Take her into the paddock." Um, there was a fence.
Mick went through the fence . . . um, John grabbed hold of her
and starting pushing her to the fence. I lifted up the wire so she
could get through. As she was going through, Mick grabbed
hold of her hair and said, "Keep your head down and don't
look at anyone."'

Using perverse and coarse language, Michael Murphy
described how various members of the group had sex or
attempted to have sex with Anita. He said he couldn't get an
erection but the others were all involved in having sex. They
stopped when they saw the lights of a car as it came down
the road. Then they dragged Anita further into the paddock.
According to Murphy, at that point they began to run away,
leaving Anita naked in the paddock.

'Um, John sang out, "Come back",' continued Murphy.
'. . . I looked back. I seen John had hold of her arm. I think
he was trying to drag her. The car went straight ahead so we
started walking back up . . . Um, she looked unconscious. And
John said, "I'm gonna cut her throat", and I said, "No, let's
leave her." John said, "No, she's seen us."

'I said, "No, come on. Leave her. She had her head down.
Leave her."

'Um, four of us started walking up the paddock, and John
went back to her. He said, "I cut her throat", running up with
blood all over him. He said, "I think I cut a couple of her fingers

off cause she put up her hand." He was big-noting about how she put her hand up. He said, "It's me first."

'Mick asked him what it felt like. He said, "Like nothing."'

Murphy said the group decided to go back to Travers's house and burn their clothes, though Travers didn't do this for some reason. Neighbours later corroborated that this took place; they remembered there being a bonfire of sorts that night.

No one will truly know what happened, as all five gave differing descriptions, particularly of their personal role in the rape and murder.

'They all said the others did it. They were and are the ultimate cowards, which I suppose was to be expected,' Kennedy told me in 2015.

Police now had confessions from all five, putting themselves at the scene of the crime. Four out of the five – all of them bar Travers – denied culpability for Anita's murder, blaming Travers alone for ending Anita's life.

Crucially, after just over twenty days of one of the most intense and public investigations seen in New South Wales, the five killers were behind bars. Everyone – from Premier Neville Wran to Police Commisioner John Avery – was heaping praise on the members of the task force for the job they had done.

After the trial, Detectives Kennedy, Rosetta and Raue would all receive commendations for their tireless work.

Graham Rosetta, for his excellent work carried out at Blacktown during this investigation and for his liaison and coordination of the police informant, which led to the arrest of the five offenders, together with the professional manner in which he conducted interviews with John Travers and Garry Murphy and [his] presentation of lengthy evidence at the Supreme Court.

Ian Kennedy, highly commended for his outstanding

leadership and devotion to duty as officer in charge of the police investigation into the rape and murder of Anita Lorraine Cobby at Blacktown on 2 February 1987. The detective sergeant's tenacity and expertise was an inspiration to the men under his charge and was instrumental to the arrest and conviction of the offenders responsible for this heinous crime.

Kevin Raue, for his excellent work carried out at Blacktown during this investigation and for his liaison and coordination of the police informant, which led to the arrest of the five offenders, together with the professional manner in which he conducted interviews with John Travers and Gary Murphy and presentation of lengthy evidence at the Supreme Court.

Awarded the Commissioner Commendation.
Signed, J.K. Avery, Commissioner

After the arrests, Kennedy declined to do any interviews, but simply gave the details to the police media unit and let them deal with the press. He insisted that the credit for catching the killers was to be shared by all those involved, and that he didn't want to be the person singled out. Kennedy even wrote a letter recommending that everyone be acknowledged in some way, from the lawyers on the case to the woman who spent hours typing up the evidence list and running sheets. 'It was such a team effort, everyone gave up their normal lives for nearly a month, with many not sleeping for days on end.' Graham Rosetta and Kevin Raue were also keen to heap praise on all the officers who were not given official recognition for the part they played in catching the killers.

Overwhelmingly, though, while proud of getting justice for the Lynch and Cobby families, they all wished the crime had never happened.

CHAPTER 9

Running from the pain

May 1986

JOHN COBBY STEPPED OFF THE PLANE from Michigan into a late autumn Sydney day. Anita had been dead four months and her killers had all been locked up.

He moved in with his grandmother Stella at Rockdale. He was broke, and too broken in spirit to work, but somehow he was still able to find money for drugs. Reality remained far too painful without a prop. By now he was also toying with changing his surname. 'I hated the Cobby name. I kept thinking people were looking at me, whispering about me, thinking I did it.'

Slowly, with his family around him, John started to ease back on the drug use. Alcohol was a different matter: he kept on drinking heavily – and continues to do so.

John had scarcely been back in the country a month when Anita's story hit the papers again, big time. A formal inquest had been dispensed with and committal proceedings for John Travers, Michael Murdoch, Michael, Les and Gary Murphy were due to start. All had pleaded not guilty. Much of what had happened to Anita had already leaked out, but for the first time the public was about to hear the full police case against these gang rapists and murderers. The committal proceedings for murders were held at the State Coroner's Court in Glebe back in the 1980s. The hearings were due to start on 23 June and were bound to re-ignite the public's morbid thirst for the details of the slaying of this beautiful young woman.

For John, ordinary things like going to the corner shop – where the newspapers were on display – or drinking at the pub – where every time he turned around he seemed to hear the words 'Anita Cobby' – caused the most pain he had ever known. He felt like he was constantly bleeding.

'I'd been back maybe six weeks when it all started up again. I had no money but I knew I had to go overseas again and get away. I sold a racehorse called Just For Jan and got $2000 for it, which thankfully was ridiculously overpriced. It gave me the cash I needed to get out of Sydney.'

John Cobby was running again . . . where would he go this time? His thoughts turned to Leonie, the girl he'd been going out with before meeting Anita.

The two had met at Sydney Hospital in 1979. For Leonie, having a male in her intake had been a novelty. She recalls, 'He was a good-looking, charismatic surfer type, passionate about things he loved and pretty popular. Although we became friends, I tried very hard not to get involved with him, as I knew he "played the field". But John can be very determined, and we did begin a relationship that lasted about eighteen months.'

The pair had a lot in common, especially skiing, cricket, horse racing and love of the beach. Leonie says that they kept their relationship secret from the other nurses in the lodge, which was a hot-bed of gossip, full of young women fresh out of school and mainly gay men.

Leonie now describes the relationship as one-sided, with John wanting commitment from her but offering none himself.

Of course, the couple were barely out of their teens, and they both knew that they had a lot of life ahead of them.

The minute John set eyes on Anita, he had been smitten.

'I do remember being with John when he first saw Anita. He was completely taken by her and embarked on a mission to have a relationship with her. I think that was the difference with her. He totally committed himself to Anita and would do anything to make her happy.'

As she relays the story of her and John to me, I sense that it must have been a painful thing to watch one of her first lovers falling totally in love with someone else. She now admits that at the time she harboured some resentment towards Anita. But there'd been no point in rivalry. It had been obvious to Leonie that John's world now revolved around Anita and that there was nothing she could do about it. When Leonie saw his reaction, despite still feeling so much for John, she moved out of the nurses' quarters. She eventually went overseas, but they had remained friends.

Leonie never completely lost her feelings for John. Not long after John and Anita had separated, on a brief visit to Australia to catch up with friends and family, she was at the races at Randwick when she spotted him and all the old emotions came flooding back.

'I was in Sydney doing some agency [nursing] work prior to leaving to go to Austria for a season in the snow. One Saturday, the girl I was going to travel with said, "Let's go to the races."'

Not long after walking through the gates at Randwick, she noticed John in the crowd and realised the attraction was still there. 'I said to my friend, "Shit, it's John . . . should I go and say hello?" Anyway, I did, and then met him later for a drink. That's when he told me Anita had left him.'

The old spark she had for John was there. While he may have left her for Anita, he had never treated her badly. She leaped at the chance to spend time with him, especially now that he appeared to be single again.

'One thing led to another, and the next day he asked me to go with him to their house, which I did. He showed me all these pictures of their life together and he was just distraught. He was already broken.'

Soon after that chance meeting, Leonie left for her trip as planned. It was while she was working as a ski instructor in Austria that she received a phone call that shook her to the core. The call was from a girlfriend in Sydney telling her that Anita had been murdered and that John was in a huge mess. The friend suggested maybe she should contact him.

But communication was nowhere near as instant then as it is now, and it took Leonie days before she was able to track John down and talk to him. When she finally reached him, the conversation was a bit awkward and she has little recall of what they spoke about. 'I think he was in a total daze,' she says. Still, they promised to stay in touch.

While there were thousands of Aussies living, working and partying in Europe, most were constantly on the move and oblivious to what was going on back home. Leonie's old nursing friends from Sydney Hospital, devastated by the murder of Anita, would send Leonie newspaper clippings, giving her a glimpse of the horror of the case and the impact it was having all over the country. Everything she heard about him on the grapevine – via the occasional phone call from mutual friends – reinforced the message that John wasn't coping well. To Leonie, it was no wonder that he had to leave Australia.

'I knew that he was getting out of Sydney and going to the US to see his mate Steven, as the media frenzy was just too much for him. He just had to get away. I had finished my season in Austria and was travelling through Europe before heading back to England while John was still in America.

'At this stage, John and I were communicating with letters, and a few phone calls. Then in May I heard from John. He had broken his ankle but was keen to come to London.'

That trip never eventuated. John headed back to Australia instead, and Leonie and John remained in occasional contact.

However, in the run-up to the committal proceedings, once again desperate to get away, John investigated his chances of getting a job with some family connections in the racing industry in England. Leonie was working in a bar called St Paul's Tavern in London and told John to meet her there when he arrived. And he did, literally: he headed straight there after getting off the plane from Sydney on 23 June, the very day the committal was due to start.

June–August 1986

Apart from confiding in his sister and a few good friends, John had kept most of his inner torment to himself. Now, meeting an old friend and ex-lover, he had found someone he could share his pain with.

'John arrived and made his way to the pub and crashed while I worked. That night after my shift we talked and drank.'

As the booze flowed, so did John's tears. 'I guess that was the first time I really heard what had happened to him after Anita's death. The moment he realised it was her on the radio in his car, his treatment by the cops, the funeral. The heroin trip. Going to the US and ending up in the looney bin.'

Leonie was struck by how bad John's physical and mental state had become. He was a lot more damaged than she had imagined from his letters and odd phone call.

'I guess my reaction was to want to care for him after going through that. Be his friend, support him, hopefully staying strong myself. The next day we walked around London and had a great day.'

For the first time since the murder, far from the manic scenes and frenzy of Sydney and the constant reminders of his life with Anita, John felt himself beginning to relax.

When I interviewed John for this book, I must confess that it made me uncomfortable to realise that he was with a woman so soon after Anita's death. For years I had carried around this image of Anita and John as star-crossed lovers separated by events beyond their control, and imagined that after Anita's death John would not have been able to be with anyone else for years. It worried me too that I was going to reveal this to the public in this book, and that readers might think less of John. As these thoughts ran through my head, I would admonish myself for being so judgemental.

When I raised the subject with John, he signalled that he wanted to hide nothing, and that this account was to be as truthful as he could make it. We had spent countless hours talking about those months immediately after Anita's death and his state of mind at the time.

'Leonie was my best friend and someone who saved me in a very dark moment,' he told me.

Then something leaped out at me as I re-read my notes about his time with Leonie in London. She was pre-Anita, and by being with her, he was back in 1979 with a young love and Anita hadn't been murdered at all. When I put my amateur psychoanalysis to John, he shrugged and said simply, 'Maybe.'

Leonie comments, 'He enjoyed the people that didn't know him and his history; he could be the old him. Yet he relied on the people that knew it all, like me. Understandable, but not always easy.'

John moved into the pub with Leonie. He was leaning on his old girlfriend both physically and mentally. He was also desperate to keep his whereabouts secret from the press. Even though he was 12,000 miles away from Sydney, he knew their tentacles could reach him anywhere, as had happened in America.

When one of the pub staff did a runner, Leonie's boss was happy to give John a go at working in the bar. He fell into the role easily, with his experience as a barman back in Sydney after leaving school.

'He was great behind the bar, and we made plans to buy a car so we could get away on weekends. At this stage I hadn't told any of our nursing friends in Sydney that John was there, as most of them had been friends of Anita's as well and I couldn't bring myself to do it.'

It was an awkward position for the young woman to be in. She had worked with Anita and was now in a relationship with her husband only a few months after Anita's murder. But there were other, unexpected stresses. Leonie comments, 'I think John was like two people in one': a mixture of the old person she knew and another man, plagued by nightmares and paranoia. 'Horrible, horrible nightmares.'

Before long, however, Leonie had a kind of reprieve from these pressures. A matter of weeks after John began pulling pints, his racing connections came through and he was offered a job as a pupil trainer at the Blewbury stables near Didcot, a couple of hours out of London. It was a genuine lucky break: it was a prestigious stable that at the time was training horses owned by the Aga Khan.

'It helped being around horses and doing something constructive,' John says. 'Also, it was a fairly isolated area, which made me feel a bit safer about people knowing who I was. I was living in the stables and then would go to a pub called the Barley Mow.'

Leonie and John would still catch up from time to time – whenever she was able to drive down to visit him. 'I was in a different world. I had no idea what I was doing, but thank God Leonie was there or else I don't think I would be here today.'

Leonie wrote a number of diary entries about John and her feelings towards him, and they are tough to read today:

14th August: David wants John to stay on at Blewbury. We had dinner at the Mischief [Pub]. John rang his mum and that night we had a 'heavy' conversation. John is depressed, having suicidal thoughts, which terrifies me. I rely on the idea that these are passing thoughts.

1st Sept: I turned 26. Spent the next day with John. Up early to see track work and a walk around the gallops. I was invited to breakfast with the Missus! Very poshy.
    At this stage I felt pulled between wanting to be with John or continue my travels with D. John suggested I stay away for a while, as he felt too attached to me and he didn't want to get fucked up by that. I began to lose my grasp on it as well. I decided to back off a bit.

8th Sept: I went to Blewbury and we went for an early morning walk on the downs. He took a sack, found a stick and proceeded to crack a couple of pheasants on the head! We sat out in the sun, plucked the buggers, took them home and deep-fried them!

On those walks on the downs, it must have felt as if the clock had been wound back and the pair were in another time, divorced from the reality of what had happened to Anita. Inevitably, though, the nightmares and John's fits of depression would bring them back to reality with a thud.

Leonie says of those confusing days: 'Despite the fun, emotionally things were getting complicated, which frightened both of us, as we weren't really in the real world with regard to everything else going on in Australia. We began making plans to either go and do a ski season in Europe or maybe I could go back to America with him. It was all a plan to stay away from the reality of things at home.'

John was keen to go back to America and asked Leonie if she would go with him. Then he received a letter from his psychologist friend Steven that mentioned some details from the committal proceedings. This stirred John up and made him think maybe he should go back home. Meanwhile, Leonie had decided to work another ski season in Austria.

'Honestly,' John tells me, 'I didn't know want to do. I was feeling better for a period of time and then bang, it would all hit me again, and then Leonie left to go to Austria. I was incredibly lonely and drinking pretty heavily I suppose, by myself at the Barley Mow.'

In the second week of October, Leonie phoned and said she was missing John. A few days later, he called her back and said he had two tickets for them to return to Australia.

Leonie had to decide whether to throw her lot in with her damaged friend or stick with her longtime travel companion, a fellow Aussie girl.

'It was an incredibly hard decision to leave my good friend. She had made up her mind to stay in Austria for the entire ski season and stuck with her plans. Leaving her was one of the hardest decisions of my life but I felt so sure that going home with John was the right thing to do. I could help and support him on his return to Sydney. That proved a fairly naïve idea.'

As Leonie puts it, things then 'went crazy'.

Acting on impulse as he often did, John had bought two tickets to Denpasar in Bali, not Sydney. In reality, the pair had very little money and the most logical thing would have been to head straight home. But essentially, John was getting cold feet and trying to find ways of delaying his return to reality.

'I am not sure what he thought would happen,' Leonie recalls. 'We arrived and found some very cheap accommodation at Legian. I have no idea how long we were there, but it didn't take John long to become incredibly paranoid. He had been there many times with Anita and seemed to think that people would recognise him and wonder why he was there with me. His fear became so bad that he told me that I couldn't come to Sydney with him, as it would all look so bad to everyone. You can imagine how I felt. It was devastating.'

Despite being heartbroken by John's decision, the ever-loyal Leonie borrowed money from her family to help John get back to Sydney without her. She also bought herself a ticket to Darwin.

'When we booked the tickets, John's flight went a day or two before mine. I can't really remember how I felt that day – numb, I would imagine. We had only spent four months together but under very extreme circumstances.

'He left and I got to Darwin with about fifty bucks in my wallet, and felt desperately screwed up.'

Leonie had been racked with guilt ever since hearing of Anita's death back in February. But the net sweeping together people and events can be cast very wide. In reality, she was another victim of this murder – someone else whose life had been deeply affected by it.

'Throughout the whole time since hearing of Anita's death and being with John, I experienced very strong feelings of guilt,' she confesses. 'I loved John, but I was only there because of what had happened to her. I used to think often of the terrible things that those men did to her. It was like she was in my head all the time too. I used to have a lot of dreams about her as well. It took a long time to rid myself of those obsessive thoughts.'

When Leonie put John on the plane in Bali, it really was goodbye. 'I have only seen John once since then in all these years. I understand now why he married Elizabeth; it was easier to be with someone who already knew about the baggage. But hey, that could have been me,' she reflects.

'All I know is now I have a nice life, beautiful kids and a great job and I wouldn't have it unless I went through all of this.'

Back in Sydney not long before Christmas 1987, single once more and working in psychiatric nursing at Garrawarra Hospital, John was trying to pick up the pieces of his life. Without much success.

The drug-taking might have stopped – and he credits Leonie with that above all – but the pattern of drinking himself into oblivion and having thoughts of killing himself was emerging again.

Ten days before the first anniversary of Anita's death, John came up with a plan. If he couldn't kill himself or the killers, he could kill off John Cobby.

On 23 January 1987, John walked into the Department of Births, Deaths and Marriages, then located at Circular Quay in Sydney. He filled in the form stating that he, John James Patrick Frances Cobby, would abandon his current surname. Then he signed it.

He walked out as a new man called John Francis. Or so he hoped.

But the ghost of John Cobby and the murder of Anita would never go away.

CHAPTER 10

The trial

Monday 16 March 1987

THE TRIAL OF THE MEN ACCUSED of killing Anita Cobby began on a Monday, at the start of a working week. Sydneysiders had an extra hour's sleep the day before after turning back their clocks for the ending of daylight savings. It was a clear, sunny day as the city's attention was centred on one of Sydney's most historic courthouses. A simple sandstone structure, it first opened its doors on 1 February 1842 as Darlinghurst Court of General and Quarter Sessions. It has long since been known as 'Darlo Court' by the lawyers, judges, police and journalists who have sat through the thousands of cases heard there.

Sydney has changed significantly since 1842. Nowadays, Darlo Court sits in the gay heart of Sydney, at the junction between Oxford Street and the beginning of the 'Golden Mile', leading to Kings Cross. Around the corner from the court, it would later be revealed, one of the defendants, Leslie Murphy, used to sell his body along the infamous Wall. Murphy was among many underage men to frequent the cash-transaction pick-up spot in Darlinghurst Road in the 1970s and 1980s.

He was also rumoured to have been a regular at a gay night-club known as Costello's, another place where underage men made themselves available for paid sex. The clientele allegedly included members of Sydney's legal fraternity, judges among them.

It was the mid-1980s, and while the gay movement was starting to make itself heard and many people had come out of the closet, a large part of society was still aggressively homophobic. 'Poofter bashing' was not uncommon. But Les Murphy's murky past wasn't the focus of the court proceedings; that would come later.

The murder case was to be heard in Court Five, the centre-piece of the six-court complex next to the old Darlinghurst police cells. Security had to be strengthened because of the still-simmering public outrage at the crime, although more than a year had passed since the murder. The worry was that someone would try to kill one of the defendants – or prosecution witnesses. All of the accused were well known in criminal circles and there was the possibility that they had associates who might be willing to do anything for the five men. Police were mindful that Travers, the ringleader, had come up with wild escape plots in the cells of Blacktown police station soon after he was arrested. Temporary metal detectors – seldom used back then – were installed outside the courtroom doors and there was a heavy police presence.

Justice Alan Victor Maxwell was the presiding judge. A former major in the Australian Army, Maxwell was sixty-five years old and known to be a tough sentencer as well as a stickler for court protocol. The defenders of the accused would be needing a lot of spine.

On the opening day of the trial, Anita's parents were there bright and early – as they would be on most mornings as the case wore on. As soon as they walked through the gates of the court complex, Kennedy briefed them on how the proceedings would unfold. He did this every time they attended the trial. On top of letting them know which witnesses were going to be called, and offering ongoing support, Kennedy was also gauging how they were coping. Even solid citizens were capable of irrational deeds. Over the course of his long career, Kennedy had witnessed the best and worst of human behaviour.

'We had to keep a close eye on the father, Garry,' said Ian Kennedy. 'Although he seemed a calm man and was a Christian, his daughter had been killed and you never know what might get into his head.'

In fact, at some point after the court case Garry Lynch admitted to me that murder had crossed his mind a number of times. 'I would only need a second to snap a neck,' he confided. 'I learnt it in the forces.'

During the investigation, Garry Lynch had said as much to Ian Kennedy. The burly detective had assured him the feelings were natural and that he understood how he felt, but urged Garry not to sink to the perpetrators' level.

The trial was set down for six weeks. The prosecution would outline their case and call about forty witnesses. The strategy would be to start with witnesses giving medical evidence of Anita's injuries, then call on the residents of Newton Road who had heard Anita's screams, and then the detectives who investigated the murder. It was planned to build to a crescendo with Miss X and the tapes, leaving no doubt in the minds of the jurors that these men were guilty beyond reasonable doubt.

But the first day of the trial started in spectacular fashion. John Travers took everyone by surprise by pleading guilty to all charges – murder, kidnapping, rape, assault, grievous bodily harm and stealing. Reporters ran for the door to file their stories for radio and newspapers. It was a dramatic beginning to what was being called the trial of the decade. The Lynches looked bewildered at the shock development.

That day the *Daily Mirror* headline screamed 'JOHN TRAVERS GUILTY'. Such was the infamy of the case that no one needed to be told who Travers was.

The bailiff then led Travers back down to the cells. For the duration of the trial, he would be held at Long Bay jail and would take no further part in the proceedings. *One down, four to go*, thought the detectives.

It was too much to expect that the others would follow suit and spare the family and friends of Anita the trauma of a long drawn-out trial. The other four had all signalled they were pleading not guilty, each blaming the others for raping Anita but adamant that the responsibility for killing her lay with John Travers. They all claimed it was his idea alone.

After a short adjournment the wheels of justice started moving again. Jury selection took up most of the morning and early afternoon. The eight men and four women were seated in the jury box as Deputy Crown Prosecutor Allan Saunders began his opening address in dramatic fashion.

He detailed the confessions the four men had made to police and then produced a large hunting knife similar to the one he said had been used to cut the throat of Anita Cobby.

'There will be no doubt from the evidence to be given to you that she was brutally and savagely murdered, and you would be less than human if you were not horrified about what you will hear in this case,' he told the jurors.

It was an impressive opening. Saunders had vividly described how a young woman had been abducted at random, raped and finally murdered.

Next the first witness was called. Anita's father, Garry Lynch, took the stand, swore the oath and, in a short but moving testimony, told the court in a slightly faltering voice that he was Anita's father and he had had to identify her body.

His strength and dignity were evident as he left the box and slowly walked past the four defendants then sat down next to his wife and held her hand.

Tuesday 17 March 1987

As the second day of the trial was about to get under way, reporters settled into their seats, prepared for a more mundane day than the first one had been. The prosecution would first call farmer John Reen to the stand to describe how he had found Anita's body.

But before the jury had even entered the courtroom, public defender Bill Hoskings, representing Michael Murphy, leaped to his feet and claimed that an article published by the *Sun* newspaper the previous day had severely prejudiced his client's chances of a fair trial.

The media's expectations of a mundane day instantly evaporated.

The late edition of Monday's *Sun* had mentioned that Michael Murphy was a prison escapee. This fact was true and widely known. However, justice is supposed to be blind – defendants are innocent until proven guilty, which is why a jury is never informed of their criminal records. Defence argued successfully that Michael Murphy would not receive a fair trial, thanks to the media coverage of his legal status.

Reluctantly, Justice Maxwell agreed and said he had no choice but to abort the trial. He discharged the jury and sent them home.

The whole process would have to restart the following Monday. Garry Lynch would have to take the stand again and publicly relive that moment when the sheet had been drawn back in Westmead morgue, revealing the battered face of his deceased daughter.

'My wife and I are as strong as whales, lions and elephants,' he told *Daily Mirror* reporter Craig McPherson the next day.

While the Lynches were being shown every consideration – and also demonstrating an astonishing capacity to confront what had happened – the contrast between them and the grieving widower couldn't have been more striking.

It was understandable that nobody in Darlo Court that day gave Anita's husband any thought at all. He had done every-thing in his power to drop off the radar: he had changed his name, was working in an isolated hospital, and had become an expert at avoiding any form of publicity. Even though John Francis was in Sydney at the time of the trial, he was keeping a very low profile. He had shaved his head to make himself even more unrecognisable.

John was aware that the trial had begun but somehow managed to keep himself away from TV, radio and news-papers. 'But I knew it was going on. The nursing staff would talk about it and I'd just try and turn off. I felt like I had two heads. I was sure people were looking at me, recognising me and whispering,' he said.

At night, even after drinking a numbing bottle of scotch, his thoughts would turn to murder, and the thoughts permeated his sleep. 'I would dream I had on a black motorcycle helmet and would burst into the courtroom with two guns blazing and kill them all. It's a dream I had for years and years. It still comes to me sometimes.'

When he recounts the part of the dream where he kills everybody, his face contorts and his hands become guns. He knows it sounds ridiculous, but it's a never-ending theme with John. Killing his wife's killers.

And during the trial he wasn't the only one with revenge killing on his mind.

Veteran *Daily Mirror* crime reporter Joe Morris was covering Darlinghurst Court at the time, as he had for the past twenty years. He was nearing eighty and had refused to take retirement; he kept turning up for work even after being given the gold watch. In the end management gave up trying to get him to retire and paid him for three days a week, although he kept working five.

A legend around the courts for decades, Joe had his own parking spot in the court complex, a privilege not even afforded to judges at the time. During the lunch break on the first day of the first trial, Joe took me aside and asked me to meet him in the car park.

We went to the back of the ageing Holden Joe owned, a former police-rounds car he had bought sight unseen when they upgraded the fleet. He opened the boot, pulled out a battered old briefcase, undid the clasp and reached inside. He then pulled out a .38 revolver and showed it to me.

'I hope one of those bastards tries to make a break for it. I'll get them, don't you worry about that, and I don't care what happens to me after.'

He closed the boot and we both went back to court. Joe didn't miss a beat. I was in awe of him and had no doubt the old bugger would have relished shooting any of them if they had come within his failing eyesight.

Monday 23 March to Wednesday 10 June 1987

A week after the first attempt to hear the case had faltered, a new jury was empanelled. The trial got under way again.

It's not a job many would relish, but the remaining four accused had the right to legal representation. In the court of public opinion, they were all as guilty as sin. Prosecutors also had a mountain of evidence against them.

Representing Gary Murphy was Leigh Johnson, a defence lawyer in her late twenties. 'It was my first big case. I was committed to my client, no matter what I thought of him. I always have and always will be.'

That couldn't have sat well with the onlookers desperate for a chance to tear her client and his associates limb from limb. 'People didn't like that and, I think, resented me for it, quite unfairly. None of the defendants were likeable. They had extensive criminal records, were not attractive to look at – in fact the opposite.' But it was her job to defend Gary Murphy, working with Canadian-born barrister Sandy Wetmore.

The atmosphere in the courtroom was charged. Every day, long queues formed outside Court Five as the public clamoured to get inside to witness the drama. 'It was highly emotional. It was not conducive to a fair trial.'

To make matters worse, the lawyers representing Gary Murphy's co-accused appeared to dislike Johnson and her partner. 'They thought we would call their clients to establish that Gary wasn't there. They were petrified they would be ripped apart by Saunders, a skilled and ferocious cross-examiner. They certainly didn't want that.'

Gary Murphy denied even having been present at the murder. Wetmore and Johnson had applied for a separate trial for him, believing it was the best chance her client had of getting off, but the application was denied.

'Maybe he wouldn't be sitting in jail for the rest of his life like he is now,' Johnson muses.

But she is pragmatic, reminding herself that Murphy, even if he was innocent of the murder, would have gone on to commit other crimes. 'No doubt he would have been in and out of prison for the rest of his life; that's one consolation. He was a career petty criminal, but I don't think he was a killer,' she says with conviction.

Johnson surprises me with her assertion that the only solid evidence against him was a statement which, she says, he signed under duress. 'He told me the only reason he signed it was because he was being beaten. He had a fractured jaw in two places, which the police said he got when he fell down some steps or something like that.'

When I raise it later with members of the investigative team, they deny the claims, saying that despite the emotion, they wouldn't have dared to physically hurt any of the accused for fear of jeopardising the case.

Ian Kennedy, especially, is adamant that police did not coerce the confessions out of the killers. He reminds me of his address to his fellow officers before they went in to arrest Gary and Michael Murphy. He had impressed upon them how important it was to stay calm, not to get carried away with the horror of what the suspects had done. 'I told them that if for some reasons these guys get off because of our actions, I would have to go and face the family. Imagine if I had to tell Grace and Garry we had the right guys but we stuffed up.' Horrified at the implications of what I have just put to him, he adds: 'Gary Murphy was injured when he ran from the house and ran into a SWOS [Special Weapons and Operations Section] team.'

At one point in the trial, Ian Kennedy, who arrested Michael Murphy, was asked how the defendant ended up with a red mark on his cheek.

'Probably when I had my foot on his head as he lay on the floor,' answered the big man.

Recently, he told me, 'It was a carpet burn, and the lawyers didn't like that answer. They were hoping for me to deny it or say I didn't know. After that they had nowhere to go. Later, Arne Tees – a legendary detective who later became a barrister – told me it was the best answer I could have given. And honest, I might add.'

When another officer was called to give evidence about the arrest and was shown the photos of Michael Murphy's injuries, the defence were still trying to prove that the mark on his face was the result of violence at the hands of police.

When he responded, like Kennedy, that the injury appeared to be a carpet burn, the defence attempted to swoop. 'The lawyer tried to be a bit of smart arse, asking the officer what expertise did he have in identifying carpet burns. He told him he had been a member of the police wrestling team for years and was very familiar with what wounds looked like when someone's face was pressed against a surface. They liked that answer less than mine.'

Kennedy brings out another story for me – about something that happened early one morning, before the courthouse was opened to the public. The trial began around Easter. In those days police were responsible for the court security, and Kennedy used to enter before the defendants were brought in; he would check on things, making sure everything was secure.

'One morning, I got there and on the dock where the prisoners sat were four little Easter eggs wrapped up in foil, sitting on the table.'

Kennedy went over to Leigh Johnson and asked who they were for. When she answered that it was Easter and that it was a small gesture, Kennedy informed her that they couldn't have them.

'I told her the wrapping was foil, which could be made into a weapon or used to try and make a device to slip cell doors or something like that, and that something could be concealed inside the eggs. I then smashed the eggs into pieces and collected the wrapping before throwing out the chocolate.'

But he didn't get all the chocolate fragments. Some lay scattered on the desk. When the accused sat down, they started to pick up the chocolate and started to eat the scraps, giggling as they stuffed the crumbs into their mouths.

'The judge was not amused. He ordered them to stop eating the chocolate.'

It had taken me a long time to persuade Leigh Johnson to open up about what she went though at the Cobby trial. When eventually she agreed to talk, in 2014, I went to meet her on the thirteenth floor of the Supreme Court building in Sydney, where she was representing a former student of the prestigious Knox Grammar private school. He was giving evidence at the Royal Commission into Institutional Responses to Child Sexual Abuse. Sadly, it was something that he had personally experienced.

'There are so many victims,' she says, before we talk about what took place when she represented Gary Murphy. She seems like the last person who would see herself as a victim, but I can't help reflecting on what a huge impact the case must have had on her life.

Because she was young and photographed well and her client was a man accused of despicable acts against a woman about her own age, Johnson was soon as big a part of the story as her defendant. It was her first experience of being thrust into the spotlight by a high-profile case, and she was totally unprepared for the intense media attention. It wasn't long before far-fetched stories started circulating among the journalists covering the case. Things like 'Johnson is in love with the guy.'

When I point out that people claimed she was flirting with Gary Murphy at the time, she responds, 'God, how could I? I spoke to him as part of my job but to say I was flirting with him was hurtful – and still is.'

For a long time, Leigh Johnson didn't realise how savage or malicious the rumours were. 'I was rung up a few years later by a journalist also writing a book, and who put it on me that I was fucking Murphy in the jail. I was furious and told her I was at the end of a 6-foot table in a glass interview room in Parklea Prison whenever I spoke to him. I threatened to sue.'

Like so many people involved in the Cobby case in different ways, Leigh Johnson has had plenty of strange encounters connected with it. It would always be when least expected that a member of the public would bring up something about it.

'In 1999 I was being photographed for an article in *Cleo*. The guy doing the photos said he went out briefly with Anita before she was married.'

At least it wasn't an angry confrontation. The harassment and accusations never seem to have stopped. 'Not long ago, I was outside a karaoke bar, near The Rocks, on my mobile, when this guy looked at me and said, "What about the Cobby killers, hey?" – really aggressively, as if I helped in the murder. Ridiculous.'

It still astounds Johnson that the rumours of her so-called romance with Gary Murphy were being spread by intelligent people. She now believes that what happened to her was the result of a deliberate and spiteful campaign orchestrated by some police and prison officers – all designed to discredit her and, by extension, her client. 'My sin was being good-looking and talking to my client – that's all – and from that I became a target for a horrible whispering campaign.'

Yet again, I wonder about the long-term consequences of the case for Leigh Johnson. From the first day of the trial, she became a celebrity lawyer in Sydney legal circles, whether she liked it or not.

'A target more like it. And I was just beginning my career.'

For six long weeks the trial went through the evidence that police had meticulously put together for Allan Saunders to present to the jury. There was no shortage of headlines as the case unravelled in the courtroom. The defence objected as more than 100 photos were put into evidence to be shown to the jury.

They were graphic, in full colour, showing Anita lying in the paddock, her eyes open, her head almost decapitated. I've seen the photos a number of times and they must surely have a deep effect on anyone who looks at them. No wonder Michael Murphy's lawyer Bill Hoskings objected; they were grotesque.

Not long into the trial the jury was taken out to the murder scene. Again, one can only wonder what the jurors were thinking as they stood at the spot where Anita's life had ended so painfully and remembered the pictures they had seen of her in that paddock. One of the jurors had to be discharged because a family member became seriously ill, so the trial proceeded with a jury of eleven.

Then there was the sight of Miss X in the witness box. She broke down several times as she recounted talking to Travers in the cell, and spoke of her fear of what might happen to her if any one of the men found out she had betrayed them. Her testimony was compelling, and irrefutably supported by the tape of her conversation with Travers in the Blacktown police cells.

Defence counsel for the four put up a brave fight, but had little ammunition in the face of the heavy artillery police had provided to the prosecution. They put forward claims of police thuggery, and of coerced confessions that they had all recanted.

They all made unsworn statements from the dock, denying they had had anything to do with the rape and murder of Anita Cobby. Each of the four was allowed to stand up in court and read out their version of events and not be cross-examined, a practice since scrapped by the legal system. Gary Murphy claimed he had got drunk that day with his brother but had left with another man, Ray Patterson, who had resprayed the car stolen by the killers. Therefore, he said, he had not taken part in the murder at all. He also said police broke his jaw during his arrest.

The other three all agreed they had been present when Anita was killed but that it was Travers who had raped and killed her. Les Murphy cried as he finished reading out his uncontested version of events.

On the morning of Tuesday 9 June, prosecutor Allan Saunders made his closing address to the remaining eleven jurors. Again he told of the last hours of Anita Cobby's life and of how she had died a horrible and slow death.

It was shortly before midday when the jurors retired to consider their verdict. The detectives and journalists waited in the courtyard, expecting a quick result. But the hours dragged on and there was no word from the jury. A few journalists went to the pub with detectives from the case.

Then, just before nine o'clock, there was movement, and the court reconvened, only to be told that there was no verdict yet. The jurors were sequestered at a nearby motel, and deliberations would resume in the morning. The Lynches went home to pass a sleepless night, wondering why the jury was taking so long.

It was an awful anticlimax. Everyone had expected a quick verdict. It was all supposed to be tied up that day. For all present, there was a deeply felt wish for it to end.

I had already written up a three-part series on the case, the centrepiece being an exclusive with John Cobby. In preparation for when the trial ended, I had also interviewed the Lynches weeks before. I had been so sure that I was set to go to press that evening with those pieces. And they had all been written on the supposition that the killers would be found guilty. That night, however, I had a sinking feeling that my supposition had been wrong, that all those words would be useless.

How could the jury not see that these animals were guilty? The thought that they might get off left me with a sick feeling in the pit of my stomach.

My thoughts turned to John. I wondered where he was and what he was doing. I hadn't had any contact with him for the past few weeks.

When we realised that the jury would need more time to deliberate and that there was no point in waiting around any longer, I headed to the Evening Star Hotel near work with a troupe of other journalists who had been working on the case. At the time I was staying at a friend's place in nearby Paddington so I could get to court early. With nothing else to distract me, I got terribly drunk.

The following morning, Wednesday 10 June, dawned clear, as it had the previous day. Once again, the media throng assembled at the court, anxiously awaiting the outcome of the trial.

At 10.20 am, the jury sent word to the judge that they had reached a verdict. At 10.40 am, the foreman of the jury rose. The judge asked how they found the charges against the accused, starting with Michael Murdoch.

Time stood still. It was like a scene in a television courtroom drama. You know the deal – how a packed courtroom falls silent, waiting with bated breath for the foreman's answer. And then it came:

'Guilty.'

A hum went around the courtroom.

In quick succession, Les, Michael and Gary Murphy were also found guilty. The relief was palpable. Everyone in the room exhaled, and umpteen journalists made a mad scramble to the door to file their stories. I raced to a *Daily Mirror* car parked illegally in the street and filed my story on a two-way radio, describing the colour of what was unfolding outside the court. There were photographers, TV crews and radio microphones all over the place. Members of the public wept openly, Garry and Grace Lynch among them.

After fifty-four days of gruelling, sometimes sickening evidence, the men who had taken the life of Anita Cobby had been publicly found to be murderers, plain and simple.

Justice Maxwell remanded the four in custody until the following Tuesday. At the appointed hour, John Travers would join them. The five would stand before Maxwell and hear how justice would be served.

That morning, at Garrawarra Hospital south of Sydney, John Francis had come off night shift at seven o'clock, returned to his small room and opened a bottle of scotch. By the time the foreman of the jury read out the word 'Guilty' four times over, the grieving husband of the late Anita Cobby was unconscious, oblivious to the dramatic scenes taking place 60 kilometres away.

CHAPTER 11

A historic sentence

Tuesday 16 June 1987

IT WAS A BLEAK WINTER'S DAY, not freezing but still with a slight chill in the air. Sydney's media were out in force to hear Justice Maxwell hand down his sentence against the guilty five.

Speculation was rife. His Honour – stiff, formal, from a distinguished legal family – had a reputation for toughness.

The judge swept into the courtroom. The preliminaries out of the way, he pulled out a sheaf of papers and began to read aloud.

Flamboyance wasn't his way. His delivery was more of a drone. Slowly and methodically, he reminded those present of the crimes committed against Anita Cobby.

Next he started with the charges against John Travers. 'The prisoner Travers was indicted before me on 16 March 1987 on five charges to which he pleaded guilty and was remanded in custody to 16 June 1987, for sentence. The charges of which he pleaded guilty are as follows.'

There they were again, those awful words: murder, abduction, assault and robbery, grievous bodily harm and rape. To these Justice Maxwell added the lesser offence of stealing a motor vehicle. Even though it was all couched in droning legalese, each word must have been like a physical blow to the Lynches, sitting quietly and expectantly in court.

The judge then went through the same process for the other four defendants. Renowned for his thoroughness, he was not about to be rushed. He kept his head down as he read, lifting it occasionally to look into the packed courtroom:

'The other four prisoners were indicted before me on 23 March 1987, on the same charges with the exception that the prisoners Michael James Murdoch, Michael Patrick Murphy and Gary Stephen Murphy were jointly charged upon the fifth charge whilst the prisoner Leslie Joseph Murphy was charged upon a separate charge of stealing . . .'

The reporters, many of whom were standing near doorways, ready to dash out to file their stories or broadcast the sentence, realised to their regret that they were in for a long wait. In the public gallery too the tension – and sense of impatience – were rising.

Seemingly in a world of their own, the five accused kept smirking and smiling at each other – as they had done throughout most of the trial. Perhaps they did not realise the gravity of the situation, that their lives were now in the hands of the stern man in the wig. Almost everyone else was on tenterhooks, conscious that this towering figure of the New South Wales judicial system had already decided their fate. All that remained was for him to let everyone present know . . . anytime soon.

Unmoved by the restlessness in the courtroom – which was betrayed by the occasional cough and the sound of individuals squirming in their seats – Maxwell ploughed on, his voice a strong monotone most of the time. Every so often, it would almost crack – and waver just a touch. But there was no lulling effect. When he recounted the crown case, Anita's family and friends needed to steel themselves.

While it was accepted, said Justice Maxwell, that John Travers had killed Anita, the other four were charged in joint purpose.

'The Crown firstly alleged that after having assaulted and robbed the deceased and sexually assaulted her by having intercourse both anally, orally and vaginally against her will, they were conscious of the fact that she could recognise them and they therefore agreed amongst themselves that she should be killed. The prisoner Travers was the one who cut her throat.

'All the others knew that Travers was armed with a knife and they contemplated that Travers would use the knife or might use the knife.'

He went on to say that the jurors were obviously in no doubt about the fact that the co-accused knew that Travers was going to kill Anita.

'She was lying face down when the prisoner Travers straddled her, pulled her head up by her hair and inflicted the fatal wounds. The medical evidence established that she was both alive and conscious before the neck wounds were inflicted.'

Silence fell in the public gallery, save for a volley of muffled sobs. But the point was not yet fully made. Grim-faced, the judge continued.

'One cannot establish precisely the length of time that she was subjected to the attacks giving rise to the wounds, bruises, cuts [and] contusions as described but it is open on the evidence to conclude that it was upwards of at least an hour and a half.'

In the backs of their minds, people knew that Anita had died a slow and agonising death, but to hear the words in open court proved devastating to many.

The true source of this devastation was not the judge but the five individuals in the dock. And now His Honour focused his comments on them. With a look of contempt, Justice Maxwell laid bare the darkness in their hearts.

'There is no doubt that apart from the humiliation, degradation and terror inflicted upon this young woman, she was the victim of a prolonged and sadistic physical and sexual assault.

'Wild animals are given to pack assaults and killings. However, they do so for the purpose of survival, and not as a result of a degrading animal passion. Not so these prisoners, they assaulted in a pack for the purpose of satisfying their lust and killed for the prevention of identification.'

After almost forty years involved in the court system, said His Honour, he had never seen a more heinous crime. And the demeanour of the killers while facing the court had further appalled him.

'Indeed, frequently they were observed to be laughing one with the other and frequently were seen to be snickering behind their hands.'

Yet it was not this apparent immaturity that drew the judge's disbelief, but the killers' absence of humanity. 'The crime is exacerbated by the fact that the victim almost certainly was made aware, in the end, of her pending death.'

The mood in the courtroom switched to anticipation. Those present were now sure the judge would show these men no mercy. Many believe that if he had had the power to do so, he would have handed down the death penalty then and there, with relish.

First the judge needed to acknowledge any submissions that might explain or mitigate in some way the actions of the accused. He noted that none had been made on behalf of Michael Murdoch and the three Murphy brothers. However, there were several submissions by Travers's defence.

To the judge's listeners, there seemed little likelihood they would have made any impression on Maxwell. In fact, he said he would not dwell on the submissions by psychiatrists Dr Hugh Jolly and Mr Geoffrey Fox, or the evidence from Miss X. He was dismissive of Dr Jolly's report that there might have been 'exculpating factors' in the murder of Anita by Travers. Jolly's assertion that 'I do not believe he acted cold-bloodedly, or reasoning in clear consciousness towards his self-preservation' was rejected outright by the judge, who said he believed the opposite: 'This was a calculating killing done in cold blood.'

By this stage, reporters from newspapers and radio were working in teams, some of them sprinting out of the courtroom to file an update while their colleagues remained inside waiting for the sentence.

Now that he had finished going through his remarks and reasons, with the tension at a high pitch, Maxwell uttered the eagerly awaited words: 'Therefore, I impose the following sentences.'

The five rose. Onlookers hoping for signs of remorse were sorely disappointed. Their sniggering continued and a couple had moronic smiles on their faces. These were the words they heard:

'John Raymond Travers, Michael James Murdoch, Leslie Joseph Murphy, Michael Patrick Murphy and Gary Steven Murphy.

'Second count, abduction: I sentence you each to penal servitude for 16 years.

'Third count, assault and rob with wounding: I sentence you each to penal servitude for 17 years.

'Fourth count, maliciously inflict actual bodily harm with intent to have sexual intercourse: I sentence you each to penal servitude for 12 years.'

Confusion reigned in the gallery until everyone realised the judge had started with some of the lesser charges and had seemed to skip over the first count. Prolonging the suspense, he moved on to the sentencing for the car-theft charge, giving Travers, Murdoch and Michael and Gary Murphy each five years; Leslie Murphy received three years. These sentences, he added, were to run from the time of their arrest the previous February.

Now, surely . . .

Once again, Justice Maxwell read out the names of the five. Whether it was intentional or not, he was extracting maximum drama from the situation.

'First count of murder: I sentence you to penal servitude for life.'

The sense of relief was overwhelming. But Maxwell was not quite finished, and as the courtroom settled, he uttered words that would make for screaming headlines that afternoon, and for years to come.

'The circumstance of these prisoners and the circumstances of the murder of Mrs Anita Lorraine Cobby prompt me to recommend that the official files of each prisoner should be clearly marked, "NEVER TO BE RELEASED".'

As the court erupted and the journalists ran to the door, the judge continued. He had some words of advice, should any government in the future think of releasing these animals: '. . . that the executive should grant the prisoners the same degree of mercy that they bestowed on Anita Lorraine Cobby in the "Boiler" paddock, Prospect, on the night of 2 February 1986. I do not think the community would expect otherwise.'

The public gallery broke into applause, began weeping or stood up before the judge ordered silence in the court.

'It was extraordinary,' says former Detective Kennedy. 'I had only seen clapping in court once before but it didn't compare to those scenes.'

The trial and sentencing of the killers were over. But not for John Cobby – or rather John Francis. He was sentenced to a life of pain, never to be released.

CHAPTER 12

Portrait of a broken man

ANITA HAD BEEN DEAD for more than two and half years, yet John was still having nightmares about her, still racked with guilt that he hadn't been there to protect her. He was still at Garrawarra Hospital, living a secret life. It was situated in Helensburgh, a small town halfway between Sydney and Wollongong, surrounded by bush, where there was little likelihood of running into any of Anita's old friends. Few people from his old world, even the cops, knew his new name. He can't even remember being told that the killers had been found guilty and sentenced.

Starting in early 2015, John and I spent hours and hours talking about his life following the murder. The problem was, there was much of it that he struggled to recall, especially during the late 1980s. Time and again, he would mention events, emotions and thoughts, only to stop and say that he couldn't be sure they were accurate because he had been heavily affected by booze and drugs. It frustrated me, yet every time we spoke we grew closer, and I became even more acutely aware of his suffering throughout those lost years of his life.

While John was in his own bubble of pain, getting by as best he could, changes were happening in the state of New South Wales that directly affected him.

Top of the list was that the state government – now under the leadership of Barrie Unsworth – introduced the Victims Compensation Scheme on 16 December 1987. Before that, victims of crime had been forced to sue in the civil court, which was a long drawn-out process and exposed the victims to cross-examination. The strict rules of evidence were seen to place unfair hardship on people who had already suffered and were attempting to gain compensation. There had also been a second option: a judge could award compensation to victims of crime and the matter was then referred to the Attorney-General to make government funds available.

After the Victims Compensation Tribunal was established in late 1987, victims could make a claim of up to $50,000. Applicants had to lodge their claim and be assessed by an accepted psychologist, doctor or other health professional. Mercifully, they did not have to attend court or face questioning, reliving their pain in public. A magistrate would then assess the medical information provided and make a judgement accordingly.

John says of the scheme, 'I had no idea it existed, and frankly wasn't thinking about getting money for Anita's death. I wanted revenge, not cash. Then Gaynor mentioned Garry had lodged an application, or was going to apply for him and Peg to get $20,000 each, and me $10,000.'

John was incensed. To him, it was blood money and he wanted no part of it. He had been holding down a steady job for the last few years and had managed to repay most of the family who had helped him out financially while he was overseas in those first few months after the murder. He was getting by.

'But Gaynor, always looking out for me, as she does, told me I should stick up for myself and deserved some compensation for what I had gone through – and was still going through – and it wasn't unreasonable for me to get half.'

It boiled inside him, but Gaynor kept at him, arguing that the money was there for him, that the scheme was for victims and he should take advantage of it. Eventually he was persuaded to make an application, although his stomach was churning as he filled out the forms. Letting others make financial decisions for you is hard to avoid when you're drifting along in an alcohol-soaked, depressive haze.

Although still hazy about many things from that period, John remembers driving north over the Sydney Harbour Bridge to a see a forensic psychologist by the name of Professor Rod Milton. On the way home, he smashed his car in the well-to-do north shore suburb of Castlecrag – memorable for all the wrong reasons.

Professor Milton was the most respected criminal psychologist in Australia at the time. Over the course of his career, he would work on nearly every high-profile murder case in Australia. He would be used as a profiler by police as they attempted to find the backpacker killer Ivan Milat.

When John and I talk over this part of his story, we both speculate about what Milton would have written about John in his report. Whatever it was, John did receive his payout. A few months after submitting his application, he received a letter that included the following:

> I have pleasure in enclosing a Notice of Determination wherein an award of compensation has been made in this matter in the sum of $25,500 plus costs in the sum of $500. It should also be noted that where claimed, medico-legal expenses are included in any award for expenses . . .

Apparently the Lynches had received a similar payment. But the letter and the money John received made him feel uneasy.

At John's urging, I decided to try to track down the report written by Professor Milton all these years later. The chances of finding such a document nearly thirty years on were going to be slim, but I inquired of the New South Wales Attorney General's Department, which had no problem with my request. 'Send in an application to view the document, if it still exists,' said a contact from the department.

So I got John to sign a letter stating that he would like to view his file from that time, and that was that. I quickly forgot about it and went on a two-week holiday.

On 28 April 2015, I was pleasantly surprised when an email from the Attorney-General's Department appeared in my in-box. Attached to it was John's file, along with the very detailed report by Rod Milton.

I hadn't given it too much thought, but I had expected that the report would contain maybe a line or two from the psychologist, and would otherwise be a routine, bland document full of pro-forma advice from a number of doctors, saying the victim was deeply distressed and traumatised due to the nature of his wife's death, etc. etc.

But Milton was far too professional and dedicated a psychologist for that. In a lengthy report, he detailed John's pain with such clarity and emotional truth that it made me cry.

In researching this book, I had found the photos of Anita dead in the paddock shocking; the autopsy report by Dr Malouf stomach-churning; and John's own accounts heart-wrenching. Somehow, that all paled in comparison to Professor Milton's report. It put beyond doubt everything John had been saying. Not only was it all true, John's portrayal of himself as a damaged and broken man had even been underplayed according to what Professor Milton reported.

In 2078 words, Milton provides devastating insight into the emotional reality of a victim of murder:

Dear Sirs, John James Patrick Cobby, aged 31 years (Dob 15/9/57)

Your reference: JEB: C25 27/1/88

Thank you for referring Mr Cobby, who attended on 27 September 1988. Mr Cobby is making a claim for criminal compensation. His wife, Mrs Anita Cobby, was sexually assaulted and brutally murdered in February 1986.

HISTORY: As a result of major emotional stress Mr Cobby does not have precise recall of many significant events in his recent life, but remembers that his wife's death took place on a Monday night. He had been out to dinner with his father and got a call from his father-on-law, Mr Lynch, to say that Anita had not come home as expected [John might have told Milton it was a call from Garry Lynch when it was in fact from his mother Terri] and asked John if he knew where Anita was. John immediately felt a sense of apprehension because Anita was extremely reliable and predictable. He suggested to Mr Lynch that the latter contact the police and check all the hospitals in the area, for this had not been done.

John then returned to his parents' home. He said, 'I knew – I knew straight away (that something bad had happened). He felt extremely anxious.

He did not go to work the next day but decided to visit his sister, who was on holiday in Gosford [Shelly Beach], in the unlikely hope that Anita had gone there. While on the way he heard a radio report that a body had been found. He imme- diately returned to Sydney. He telephoned the Lynches from Hornsby and was to go at once to their home. The family was sitting in the backyard and he joined them. The police were in attendance and requested that someone come to identify the body. He felt himself unable to do so, saying 'I don't know why. I'm a nurse. I see bodies all the time but I couldn't bear to see Anita.' The police said she was 'very gory, very bloody' and suggested that Mr Lynch go because he did not seem so affected.

John was taken back to the police station to make a statement. He remembers feeling dizzy and sick and having to lie on the floor. He was shocked and in a state of disbelief. He was questioned aggressively and found this extremely upsetting because it seemed he was a prime suspect.

He could not eat or sleep. He felt totally alone. He thought constantly of Anita's suffering, of her being alone when being assaulted and killed. He imagined her calling out to him. He had a mixture of panic and anger, wanting to help her but being unable to do so. He felt guilty, blaming himself for not having picked her up that night, although he remembered her having told him not to do so because she was dining with friends. He could not return to work. He was afraid of being seen in public because of the extensive news coverage of the event. He was upset with his father-in-law, who seemed to handle himself too well and did not show much emotion. (He eventually withdrew from his in-laws, although previously he had been extremely close to them.)

Mostly he just wanted to escape. He wanted to forget everything that had happened but was unable to do so. He had nightmares every night. He would imagine himself taking revenge on Anita's killers. He imagined he could hear her screaming and clawing her attackers and trying to escape. He felt angry, impotent, and hopeless. The dreams came 'every time I'd nod off' and he began drinking to excess, 'heaps and heaps so I could go to sleep without dreams'.

Two days after the funeral he left Sydney to reside with an

old school friend living in the United States. His friend was a psychologist and tried to help John by counselling and relaxation therapy; but this was inadequate. His friend arranged for him to be admitted to a psychiatric hospital, the Pontiac General, but he found the experience frightening because there were many obviously disturbed patients in the ward. He pretended he was better in order to be discharged. He resided with his friend for the next few months, and drank constantly during the time – about a bottle of whisky every night in order to get to sleep. His friend gave good support.

He continued distressed after his return, although less than immediately after the funeral. Unfortunately, the event again assumed prominence in the newspapers, perhaps because of the committal hearing or trial, and his symptoms returned with the same intensity. He left Australia again, this time to go to the United Kingdom, where he worked for a racehorse trainer whom he had known in Australia. He was away five months, returning about the end of November 1986. The event was out of the news by this time and he felt he could start to rebuild his life. He said, 'The whole time, all I wanted to [do] was just run away'.

In February 1987 he took a job at Garrawarra hospital at Waterfall in the [Royal] National Park. He lived in the nurses' home and had a quiet and secluded existence. Unfortunately, there were further headlines in the papers, and on one occasion his photograph was published. His sense of peace and seclusion disappeared but he continued to stay there. He continued to drink to excess and after a time felt he was going out of his mind. He saw a general practitioner. He was hospitalised. Alcohol was withdrawn and he was placed on a mixture of anti-depressants and a beta-blocking agent, with considerable improvement. He began to sleep better and no longer took alcohol or some sedatives which had been given to him earlier.

The nightmares have largely ceased now but he is still unable to [get] the fantasies of Anita's death out of his mind, nor his preoccupation with her death and revenge for it. There is a persistent feeling of impotence and guilt.

He remains socially withdrawn. He used to go to the races (his father is a bookmaker) but cannot go into the members' stand now because he thinks people will look at him and remark on his presence. He maintains good contact with his parents and has a friendly relationship with his workmates. He has had occasional relationships with young women but these never come to anything.

He said, 'I just can't love now – I just feel cold.' His interests are rather restricted. He still maintains a lifelong interest in racing but nothing much else. He used to love swimming and exercising but cannot seem to raise an interest in them now and feels generally lethargic and out of touch. His concentration is improving.

BACKGROUND: Mr Cobby was born in Sydney, where his father, aged 56 years, continues to work as a bookmaker. His mother works in the TAB. He has a good relationship with both parents and his 26-year-old sister.

He attended Waverley College, completed his Higher School Certificate and then began nursing at Sydney Hospital. Anita was a couple of years behind him. She appealed to him because of her warmth and kindness, and they had an excellent and close relationship. He thinks they married about 1982 but cannot remember the year definitely.

PRESENTATION: He gave a good account in a reserved fashion and showed little emotion. He seemed to [be] doing his best to suppress intense feelings of loss, grief, anger and impotence.

OPINION: Mr Cobby suffered a severe post-traumatic stress reaction as a result of the killing. He continues to remain socially withdrawn and is unable to get the terrible experiences out of his mind and get on with the rest of his life. He is largely incapable of close relationships now. His interests are limited. He suffered a severe alcohol problem in which he took alcohol for symptomatic relief but recovered from this problem under the skilled care of a doctor. He was driven to change his name in order to avoid untoward interest from others.

The prognosis is guarded. He has a good personality but the stress to which he was exposed was extreme and he is likely to be reminded of his experiences by further publicity from time to time. There will most likely be an enduring problem forming relationships. I suggested that, in addition to continued counselling services, he see if he can make contact with a priest who can offer additional support (John was raised as a Catholic, had comfort from his beliefs earlier, and might well be able to again in the future).

Yours faithfully,

Rod Milton

Another report was attached to John's file, much shorter and nowhere near as extensive as Milton's. However, here was another professional painting the same picture:

Mr Cobby is absolutely devastated since Mrs Cobby's death. He was, prior to this event, a well-adjusted, outgoing, social, sport-loving etc person.

He is now a recluse, depressed, with a severe alcohol problem – eg a bottle of scotch per day, has enormous quantities of pills, tranquilisers, sedatives, hypnotics, pain relievers etc.

He had to leave the country on two occasions to escape and has left the state on a further occasion.

He has incapacitating migraines. He wants to run again. I am most concerned about his present state of health and his future. He has suffered greatly.

Yours faithfully,

Dr Bernard R. Kelly

The report and file were sent to me at the end of April 2015, twenty-seven years after they were written. After reading them, I went back to the tapes of our interviews and was struck by how closely what John had said to me mirrored what he had told Professor Milton back in 1988. There were some slight discrepancies – his memory playing tricks on him – and in 1988 John had obviously held back his flirtations with heroin and cocaine.

When I brought up this omission with John, he said that although Professor Milton made him feel very comfortable, he was deeply embarrassed about his drug use – and still is – and chose not to reveal it. 'It was the lowest of lows in my life,' he said.

Interestingly, John ran into Professor Milton in 2001 at a medical conference in Bondi. John was there as part of his ongoing career development; he decided to switch from general nursing to psychiatric care three years after Anita's murder when he was working at Garrawarra Hospital.

'I went up to him after he spoke and introduced myself as John Cobby and said he probably didn't remember me but we had spoken years before. He looked at me, said, "Of course I remember you, but I'm surprised to see you. Honestly, I thought you would be dead or curled up on a park bench." He was gentle when he said it to me, but it was a pretty mind-blowing thing to hear.'

That expression 'mind-blowing' preyed on my thoughts. I

sat on the report for weeks before I revealed to John that I had it, even when he pestered me, asking me if I had heard back from the authorities. If I had found it confronting to read, I reasoned, surely it was going to take John back to some of his worst moments and cause him to re-experience that pain. And even though he had relived a lot of it during interviews with me, it was another thing to see it all laid out in black and white by a psychologist.

Another thing that had shocked me in the report was the bit about the dreams. When John had talked to me about the dreams he had, and still has, about Anita, he had never conveyed their intensity – how Anita would be screaming for him, or how he would see her fighting for her life while she was being attacked.

John kept asking me to give him a print-out of the report, particularly curious to know what Milton had said about him after their session, because he never saw the report at the time. In the end, when I looked at it from his point of view, it was obvious that it was his right to see it. Getting hold of the report had been his idea, after all.

Taking a deep breath, I made arrangements to hand him a copy in person. Fresh from discussing my misgivings with his sister, I met John at Bronte Beach one Saturday.

My plan had been to stay with him while he read it, which Gaynor thought was a good idea, but John was adamant that he would be okay to read it on his own. Basically, he refused point-blank to read it while I was there.

Reluctantly, I agreed and suggested that he read it then go out into the surf. It was something that always seemed to give him solace. He looked me in the eye and nodded.

As I walked away from him, I felt churned up. Back at home, I poured myself a beer and tried without success to work.

A couple of hours passed and then John rang me. It was about two o'clock.

'Fuck. Pretty confronting, isn't it? . . . I was a pretty sick puppy back then,' he added, trying to put on a bit of bravado. 'Why didn't I just top myself?'

It was hard to know what to say. I told him I'd already had a couple of beers, just thinking about what he was going to read.

'Well, I've had a couple of wines myself and I reckon I'm going to have a lot more now.'

It was understandable, and in many ways I would have liked to have joined him. In the two months since we had started writing the book, John and I had been in contact almost daily.

But I wasn't going to get plastered that night. Instead, I was going to dinner with my wife, Nicole, and I told John that.

'You go to her and you love her as hard as you can. Give her the love I couldn't give Anita,' he said before hanging up.

CHAPTER 13

Elizabeth

1986–2002

IT WAS 31 DECEMBER 1986, John's first New Year's Eve without Anita. Resolutions? There was not much he genuinely wanted to do except maybe commit suicide, a thought that had been with him since she died. Somehow, though, he was still alive, despite the booze and drug binge he had embarked upon immediately after her death.

His sister Gaynor was desperately trying to get some normality back into his life. Seeing John come back from the United States a total train wreck, almost unrecognisable, had shocked her. She had realised that his life would never be the same again – hers either – but she refused to accept that the big, strong older brother she had adored since they were kids was gone for good.

Heartened that he seemed to be off the drugs and improving slightly when he first came back from England, Gaynor witnessed her brother becoming more and more withdrawn from his friends and even his family. He began a lifetime practice of avoiding celebrations such as birthdays, Christmas Day and New Year's Eve, always volunteering to work at whichever hospital was currently employing him.

But Gaynor Cobby, four years younger than John and also grieving the loss of her good friend and sister-in-law, was determined to fight her way out of her own sadness and take John with her. As New Year's Eve approached, she arranged to party in Sydney's Rocks area with a few friends at a restaurant–bar called Phillip's Foote. It was a raucous place, frequented by young office workers from the city. In the lead-up to New Year's Eve, Gaynor started a campaign to get John to go with her, basically nagging him in a nice way.

'She was and has always been there for me. The murder hit her hard too, because Anita and her were such good friends, and I know she was trying to help me. I didn't want help, didn't want to go out, didn't want to see people, but I could see how hard she was trying.'

To please his sister, John reluctantly agreed to go along for a couple of hours in the early evening. He was rostered on to do a shift from 11 pm to 7 am at Concord Hospital's burns unit, not wanting to celebrate the incoming New Year that year or any other. There was nothing to look forward to, as far as John was concerned.

When he arrived, people were laughing and smiling all around him, which made him feel more uncomfortable. 'I was pretty paranoid at that time.'

Frankly, he was now unrecognisable from the man Gaynor's friends had known before Anita's death. His hair had thinned and his body had taken on an almost emaciated look.

Gaynor and her pals were warming up for midnight. John sat on a beer, feeling awkward. Then his sister introduced him to her friend Elizabeth, a law clerk. Gaynor had gotten to know Elizabeth through a boyfriend she was dating at the time.

John and Elizabeth had met before. It had been at a concert by UK band The Police in 1984, and John had been with

Anita. Elizabeth was well aware of John's story and knew what a bad way he was in.

Elizabeth and John chatted for a bit before John went on his way to work the lonely graveyard shift he had gone out of his way to land that night. Today he has no idea what he did at midnight.

By now John's life revolved mostly around his work at Garrawarra Hospital. He was virtually a recluse, living quietly in the nurses' quarters, which were tucked away in peaceful bushland. There, he could work hard, then drink himself into oblivion on his days off. John had thought about giving away nursing, but other than horses, it was really the only thing he knew. And he had to earn money. His focus was on repaying the last of the money he had borrowed from friends and family in those six months after Anita's death.

'When I got back to Australia the second time, I think on the surface I would have appeared kind of normal to people that didn't know me, or perhaps just a bit of an idiot. I would shave my head, let it grow and then dye it. But the dreams at night were constant, as well as the guilt and grief.'

He rejected any suggestion by family and friends that he should get counselling, seeing it as a weakness. When he tells me this, my eyebrows shoot up. John shrugs and says he grew up in an era when men didn't seek help.

'And besides, Steven had tried to help and it didn't work. After going into that psych ward in America, I was worried I would be committed to some lunatic asylum. There was no way I was going to risk that.'

At the beginning of March 1987, Gaynor made another concerted attempt to get her reclusive brother to come out with her. She was organising a group of friends to meet for drinks at the Five Doors restaurant in Cleveland Street, Surry Hills. As with the New Year's Eve gathering, she chipped away at John, constantly bringing it up and persuading him he'd enjoy himself.

'I was trying to get him out to socialise. He was just so sad, and I hated seeing him that way,' Gaynor recalls.

'I went along basically to make Gaynor happy and stop her pestering me,' says John. 'Elizabeth was there and we started talking and I felt a connection with her. It was the first time since Anita's death that I had felt anything real for another living soul. I was so wrapped up in my own grief that I couldn't let anyone in, even Leonie, who had tried so hard. I wanted to be a normal guy again but my heart wasn't in it.'

John remembers that he drank a lot that night, and the next thing he knew, he and Elizabeth were in the back of a cab kissing. He felt all sorts of emotions, liking the touch of someone he had a rapport with but still feeling scared and guilty, especially now he was back in Sydney, where he was surrounded by memories of Anita. In London with Leonie, his mind had divorced itself for a short time from the pain he was feeling.

'Really, I couldn't be with anyone properly because I was so scared it would be taken from me. Even today I have that feeling, but here was someone so pretty and someone I started to feel truly comfortable with.'

He spent the night with Elizabeth and the next day the pair went to the races. Over the next few months they saw a lot of each other, and soon began a steady relationship.

'I was trying to get on with things, and Elizabeth was a wonderful person who gave so much of herself to me. She knew what had happened, knew Anita and was close to Gaynor, but we never really discussed what had happened in depth. I suppose it was the elephant in the room but we kept seeing each other.'

For all of 1987, throughout the trial and afterwards, the relationship followed a stop–start pattern, where John would draw closer to Elizabeth for a while, then he would distance himself. In the back of his mind was the dread that if he became close to someone, they would be taken from him, like Anita had been.

John was working seven days on and seven off. Often, if things were going well, on his week off he would travel to Elizabeth's house in Erskineville, in Sydney's inner west, and stay with her. But then there would be weeks of remaining in his room at the hospital in deep depression.

'That must have been so hard for her,' John observes. 'My behaviour was totally erratic but I was fighting emotions about Elizabeth. I felt I needed someone, and Elizabeth was truly amazingly patient with me. I was creeping up to thirty and thinking maybe it was time to think about a family. That's what normal people do and that's what I wanted to be. Normal.'

He knows now how damaged he was and is astonished that she got mixed up with him. 'But she wanted to save me from myself and truly thought she could. Elizabeth told me years later, when I asked her why she married me. She looked at me and said, "I thought I could fix you."'

Gradually, despite John's conflicts about commitment, the two fell into a quasi de-facto relationship. By then Elizabeth, who was six years John's junior, was working as an airline hostess.

For John's part, he felt he owed Elizabeth some stability after all the support she had given him, constantly putting up with his fragile state of mind. On 16 December 1989 the couple married in St Carmel Church in Waterloo. John's sister, mother and grandmother witnessed what they hoped would be a new beginning for John, a return to the carefree young man they had seen growing up.

Following the pattern of John's wedding to Anita, his father was not invited. Their relationship had been strained for years, but any chance of reconciliation had disappeared when he had a massive fight with his father on the way back from Kembla Grange races one day.

'Dad was filthy with me for changing my name – really, really dirty about it – and he blew up. I got him to stop the car and walked the rest of the way home to Garrawarra Hospital, probably about 10 kilometres away at least. You have got to realise it was all about me. Even those close to me meant nothing. I was a selfish c—,' he says with unflinching honesty.

After the wedding, John moved into Elizabeth's home in Ashmore Street, Erskineville. Sometime later they moved to nearby Canterbury, where John started training horses, as well as continuing with his nursing. Elizabeth decided to take on a new career as an air hostess. Life became far more settled.

John describes those early years with Elizabeth as magical. They went a long way towards helping him cope with what was still gnawing away at him.

Working with horses was also therapeutic. 'We had seven horses, and stables in the backyard, and they were going well. I had a few Sydney metropolitan winners,' he says proudly. Sticking to his adage of never putting money on anything he didn't train, John won some decent sums of money backing his own horses.

When the couple welcomed their first child, a daughter named Aerin, in February 1993, it appeared that John Francis had at last turned a corner. Anyone who saw the Francises would have been envious. A good-looking couple with a beautiful daughter. They were living in a huge house at Canterbury and had plenty of money. He was a successful horse trainer; she was leading a glamorous life as an air hostess.

'But I admit Anita was still there in the back of my mind. Elizabeth was so stoic and tough and I was a selfish prick, totally wrapped up in myself. I wasn't a good person to live with. I was a horrible, horrible person, I reckon.'

John was still drinking heavily, to mask his depression and

the spectre of Anita in the background of what seemed to be a successful marriage. 'I can't remember ever talking to Elizabeth about Anita with any real sort of feeling at any time in the marriage, although she might remember differently.'

On 2 September 1996, their son Daniel was born and things seemed okay. With a son to complement his beautiful daughter, John's nuclear family was complete. But he continued to grapple with depression – and make a good fist at hiding it most days.

Then something happened that undid all the healing. It was as though lightning struck.

When Daniel was a toddler, still in nappies, John accidentally ran over his son, trapping him under the rear wheel of his car at his stables at Canterbury.

'I totally panicked and tried to lift the car off his leg, absolutely distraught. He was pinned by the car. Then I got in the car and drove it off him.'

Miraculously, Daniel had no lasting injuries at all, not even a scratch, but the incident traumatised John to the point where he went into a deep depression and couldn't go to work. All he was doing was drinking and staying in bed. In the blink of an eye, someone he loved had been hurt, and once again he was brought to his knees.

'When I first saw Daniel under the car, I thought he was dead, even though he was probably wailing. Soon I started having thoughts that I'd killed Anita and now my kid. It totally took me back to square one about Anita, for some reason.'

Before he could return to work, his bosses and workmates made him go to a counsellor, something he had avoided for so many years. During one of the early sessions, the counsellor turned to him and said, 'There's something else going on here. This isn't about the accident, is it?'

With that, the floodgates opened. John blurted out the secrets from his background, telling the counsellor about Anita and the years of trauma that had followed. It was obvious that

Anita's murder was still seriously affecting him.

When the counsellor coaxed out of John the fact that he had not been back to Anita's grave since the funeral in 1986, the next thing John knew, the counsellor was driving him out to Minchinbury to visit the grave site. That was the first time he truly accepted that she was gone from the earth.

'It was a funny feeling. I felt that Anita wasn't here anymore. I know it sounds weird and a bit out there, but it's exactly the way I felt. I knew she was gone.'

But after the three weeks of enforced sessions with the counsellor, John stopped seeing him. It was a repeat of his session with Professor Milton in 1988: he only saw psychologists when he had to. He admits now that maybe if he had stuck with it, he might have been able to cope a little better with the torment he put himself through for years. But he is stubborn by nature and had convinced himself that he was totally beyond help. Who knows – perhaps the self-loathing was a way of punishing himself for failing Anita; perhaps there was a part of him that felt he didn't deserve to have any peace of mind.

In the short term at least, the few sessions had worked a treat. John was up and about again. It appeared that he was able to move on from the incident with Daniel that had set him back so badly. And if he was putting on a front, no one would have picked it.

His horses were going from strength to strength. Surprising all those who knew him well, John even did a couple of newspaper interviews about his success as a trainer, and was quoted in articles in Sydney's *Daily Telegraph* and the *Sydney Morning Herald* in 1997.

'By then I had been John Francis for ten years and when the reporters came up to me, I kind of just went, "Why not?" No one knew who I was, and I got away with it.'

*

As the saying goes, the only constant in life is change. That same year, Canterbury stables were closed down as a training facility for horses and the Francis family moved to Malabar, back to John's eastern-suburbs roots.

Until then, John had been working on and off, temping at hospitals and spending a lot of his time training horses. Now, with two children to feed, he was looking for a steady job.

Just three streets from where they had set up home was Long Bay jail, complete with a hospital wing.

'For a nurse, it was the easiest place in the world to get a job. There were always vacancies, as you would expect. It's pretty hard-core work, and dealing with all kinds of low-lifes and some very sick people.'

To me, it seems a strange place to seek employment when you were once the husband of a high-profile murder victim. When I suggest it could have been a subconscious attempt to find out where his wife's killers were and try to extract revenge, John dismisses the possibility. Bluntly, I ask whether the management had any idea of his background when he went for the job.

'Shit, no,' he says. 'I didn't tell them or else I would never have got the job. Honestly, it was around the corner from home and was pretty easy work – clock on, clock off – and there was a loading because of the people we were dealing with. It's as simple as that.'

When I take up the subject with his sister, even she – his biggest supporter over all these years – isn't convinced John was motivated purely by convenience.

'He wanted to kill them and I think that's why he worked there. More than once after Anita's murder he told me he was going to commit a crime, go to jail to find them and kill them. It would have been at the back of his mind for sure,' Gaynor says.

John does admit he was looking on patient lists for names he might recognise, even though he wasn't certain of the offenders' names. He was also listening in on prisoners' conversations in case he picked up some information about his wife's killers, but he never did, and he repeatedly rejects the idea it had anything to do with his taking the job at the jail.

'Although I wondered, if ever I were to come across one of them, could I kill them? I don't know. I want to, crave doing it, but don't know if I have the courage.'

A few months after he started work at the jail, his original identity as John Cobby was discovered by management – as it was from time to time over the years, at different places where he worked.

'I don't know how, but it got out. But the deputy governor at the time was terrific. He pulled me aside one day and said he would make sure none of them [the killers] would be there while I was working there.' Conscious, too, that a lot of the people he came in contact with inside the prison were sociopaths, he was careful never to let on to his patients who he was.

So much for what might have been, and never was. Regardless of what had brought him there, it still surprises me that he would end up working in an institution that housed some of the state's worst criminals. After repeating that it was a job and he needed money, John concedes it probably does seem odd, even bizarre . . . And then out tumble a couple of stories.

In the hospital wing, he struck up a relationship with killer and convicted rapist Neddy Smith, probably one of Sydney's most dangerous men in the 1980s. 'We talked occasionally, mainly about horses. He was a mad punter and somehow was able to follow the races inside. We would chat about whether a horse was a good thing or not. Neddy was a huge, strong man. Quite frightening really.'

Another time he remembers meeting Louis Bayeh of *Underbelly* fame, the one-time boss of Kings Cross. 'I had a

$20 note in my top pocket showing through my uniform and he just kept staring at it. It was really strange, his total preoccupation with a twenty-buck note.'

Not all the inmates he treated were big names, but some were pretty scary. 'One guy was in there for cutting off the heads of two people with an axe. He wasn't a monster; he was truly a sick person.'

I'm bewildered when he tells me this, laying bare the contradictions of John Cobby. Here was a man full of hatred for the individuals who had killed his wife, yet working in a prison and helping convicted killers, even sympathising with some of them.

Puzzled yet again by what I am learning about John, I turn for comment to his sister Gaynor.

'Deep down, John is a kind soul and a nicer person than he gives himself credit for,' she says. 'How could you be a nurse for over thirty years, helping sick people, taking care of them, and be as horrible a person as he thinks he is? There is a caring side of him he doesn't even recognise himself.'

John worked at the jail from 1997 to 2003, while he and Elizabeth brought up their two children. They never mentioned anything about Anita to Daniel and Aerin. On the outside, everything seemed fine, but John knows he subjected his family to wild mood swings and was still drinking heavily.

He always loved his children and has a fantastic relationship with them now. 'But I don't think I was a very good father. I was probably a cranky bastard.'

When I talk to his son, Daniel, now travelling the world as a caddy for Jake Higginbottom, a promising young Australian golf player, he says his dad was pretty normal, although perhaps a bit over-protective.

'But I know now why. Dad would take me to my footy matches wherever I was playing, but not if it was out west or especially near Blacktown. Mum would have to do those games. It makes sense now.'

Something peculiar happened when Daniel was about four-teen. He and his father were watching television at home in Malabar when a promotion for a crime show came on the screen and up flashed the face of Anita Cobby and the five convicted killers.

'Dad stood up and just pointed and yelled, "C—. C—. C—."'

It was totally out of the blue and shook Daniel up. A few days later, his dad sat him and Aerin down and told them about Anita. John says Elizabeth was furious with him for doing this, but he felt it was time to let them know.

'I didn't know anything about the murder then, but since then I have looked it up on the internet,' said Daniel. It shocked the teenager to know his father's first wife had been the victim of such a high-profile murder.

Things about his background started to fall into place for the teenager. Simple things, like why his cousin was called Cobby and he wasn't.

'It had always seemed strange then. It's only now, with talking to Dad about everything, that I can put it all together.'

What was sad was that by the time John told his children about his murdered first wife, his marriage of sixteen years to their mother was falling apart.

'For a while, everything was great, especially in those early days, then the kids came along and you refocus your life. Then the training facilities at Canterbury were closed down and that was a real blow to me. They wouldn't let me train at Randwick. You needed to have a lot more influence than I did to get a spot there. I was offered Rosehill or Warwick Farm, but knocked it back. My roots have always been in the eastern suburbs. Maybe I'm a snob, but it's where I grew up and feel comfortable.'

Things seemed to deteriorate after John was no longer training horses. The work had helped give him a direction in life – that and his family – and without it he didn't do as well. Money pressures started to grow after they moved to Malabar and embarked on expensive renovations.

In 2005, Elizabeth and John decided to split. For over seventeen years Elizabeth had stood by and watched John try to slowly kill himself with booze and self-hatred.

There's no one issue that John can see led to the break-up, but he believes it was his depression that finally got the better of his wife.

'It was fairly amicable, and Elizabeth never stopped me seeing the children, which I am eternally grateful for.'

The woman who had tried so hard to save John from himself was now gone. She kept the family home and he moved into an investment property in the neighbouring suburb of Hillsdale, which the couple had purchased when things were going well.

The nuclear family had been an anchor for John for so many years and the anchor had now been pulled up. He was feeling desperately alone, cut adrift, but religiously kept in touch with his children.

'Although I saw them a lot, it wasn't the same as being in the same house as them. When you are not around them constantly, you miss them terribly.'

Things really fell apart again when John injured his shoulder at work and had to undergo a major reconstruction, preventing him from working or surfing. The old John returned: he spent days in a deep fog, taking huge amounts of pain-killers like OxyContin and Endone, and at the same time drinking heavily. Not a good mix for someone already feeling depressed.

'It was really like going back to those dark days after Anita died, where I just didn't give a stuff about myself or what I was doing to my body.'

But every time John has fallen into despair, someone has come along and given him a reason for living. This time it was his daughter Aerin.

His face lights up like a Christmas tree when he talks about taking Aerin, then aged sixteen, on a European holiday in 2008, which brought them closer together. 'Dan was caught up with his mates and his sport and didn't want to come, so Aerin and I took off to Europe for a fantastic two months.'

Father and daughter started off in London then went to see some schoolfriends of Aerin's who had relocated to Ireland. 'We saw Bono in Grafton Street, Dublin, and went up and got our photo taken with him, which was a blast. Probably more for me than Aerin,' he says, smiling.

When they visited Rome, Anita's favourite city, and located the Trevi Fountain, John felt her presence.

'That afternoon, after visiting the fountain, we were sitting at the same railway station on the same seat where I was with Anita twenty-three years before. It was kind of eerie.'

But a bigger coincidence was in store for John when he and Aerin went on to Florence. They were wandering the streets doing nothing in particular when they stumbled upon a bronze statue of a pig in a fountain. *Il Porcellino*, or 'Little Pig', was located at one side of the New Market. Local legend has it that if you rub the pig's nose, you will have great luck and will return to Florence.

John could hardly believe his eyes. 'The statue is an exact replica of one at Sydney Hospital, where Anita and I worked together. She was forever rubbing its nose and laughing about the luck it would bring us.

'It totally blew me away. I had no idea it was there and I got a bit emotional. I think at times Anita is following me and I honestly believe her spirit was there that day and she was looking at us and smiling.' While he knows it sounds a 'bit out there', John has long believed in the spiritual world, a belief he shared with Anita.

Within a few months of coming home, Aerin told her dad she wanted to go to Trinity College in Dublin to study to become a doctor. Whereas many parents would have scoffed, John moved heaven and earth to make his daughter's wish come true. He spent months getting accreditation so he could work as a registered nurse in Ireland and mortgaged the home in Hillsdale that he had bought with his divorce settlement.

Just before Christmas in 2008, John and Aerin took off for Ireland so she could chase her dream. John wasn't in love with the idea of leaving Dan or even living in Ireland but he wanted to make his daughter happy. He enrolled her into Loreto Abby, Dalkey, an expensive Catholic girls' school, where he hoped she'd receive a good enough education to get in to Trinity.

'But after seven weeks, Aerin was missing Australia, her friends and her mother and wanted to go back. I was locked into a contract where I was working, so Aerin went home and I spent the next six months in Ireland, totally miserable. It was freezing cold, black ice storms and away from the kids.'

As soon as he could, John returned to Sydney. The Prince of Wales Hospital, where he'd worked after leaving Long Bay, put him on staff immediately. He moved into the nurses' quarters and started all over again.

But John has no regrets about having chased his daughter's dream with her, no matter how short-lived. 'It's what you do as a parent, I guess,' he says.

He soon bought a small flat in Bronte and started living alone again. For the first two years after his marriage collapsed he had kept to himself, staying away from any form of commitment. He was now working in the psychiatric wing of Royal Randwick Hospital as a senior nurse. His children and his sister Gaynor were effectively the only people he saw outside of work, apart from locals in the surf at Bronte.

His life was now simple and lonely, but he had his children. Family life and Elizabeth had saved him from killing himself in those years after Anita's death. Despite the fact the marriage was over, he knew how vital Elizabeth had been to him: she had given him Aerin and Daniel, and the knowledge that he was not beyond feeling unconditional love, that he had a reason to live.

Then, in 2011, he was talking to a young nurse, Jane, telling her about his love of the surf. Blonde, attractive and a bit of a loner herself, she told John how she had always wanted to surf. John is obsessed with surfing and can't understand why the whole world doesn't share his passion, so when Jane showed an interest he quickly asked her if she wanted to have a lesson.

Three mornings later they met at Bronte Beach and spent hours surfing in the warm February water. For John there were no thoughts of becoming romantically involved with a woman a lot younger than him.

'But that day there was a connection which was really nice to have, more of a friendship. I was so much older and she was young. I was just an old guy teaching her surfing.'

The relationship developed and it wasn't long before they began to see each other, spending hours talking about their lives.

'Jane had no idea of my past and even though she knew about the murder of a nurse called Anita Cobby, she didn't know any of the details. I kept it that way for a few months.'

Then, as he began to feel closer to her, his need to confide in her his secret burden grew. Finally he decided to tell her about Anita.

'She took it pretty well and was quiet for a long time, I suppose there isn't much she could say.'

When I point out that he is now in a relationship with a nurse who is about the same age as Anita was when she died, he scoffs at any suggestion that it is a subliminal attempt at reliving his life with Anita.

Jane, a quiet and introverted woman, will only talk about the John she knows now and won't dissect their relationship. For both of them, it is just a simple bond of friendship, which happens every day, all over the world. She doesn't talk much about Anita or how she felt when John told her about his former wife, but comments that those tragic events go a long way towards explaining some aspects of his behaviour.

'He screams in his sleep. It's worse if he is alone and I hear him if I am watching TV or something and not next to him. While he is asleep, his hand always searches the bed to find me. If ever he can't find me, he wakes up in a panic,' she says.

According to Jane, he will sometimes go for days without eating and he can sleep for an entire weekend when he gets depressed. And every now and again he will take himself away from Sydney for days. 'John has very low self-esteem and fakes this type of bravado to cover it.'

But as she saw more of John and their relationship deepened, she was also able to see a lovely side of John that he himself will never acknowledge.

'He fights battles for people and can be incredibly generous and kind. In the workplace, the women seem to naturally flock to him because of his sympathetic nature. He stands up to authority if he thinks someone is being bullied.'

Fairly recently, she found out that John had been buying gluten-free products for a patient out of his own pocket: surprising behaviour for someone who describes himself as totally self-centred.

'John runs away to Indonesia as his way of coping. He told me he loves to go there because no one knows him, and his persona completely changes the moment we touch down.

'It's a different John, carefree and running around making everyone happy. He drinks maybe a bottle of beer a night . . . When we leave, he gives away his clothes and surfboards to the locals.'

Then Jane shares with me something John has forgotten to mention – or perhaps has been hiding from me.

'About a year ago [2014], John went to apply for a job at Long Bay jail again, but I discouraged him and I think he realised that they would probably know who he was this time.'

John again denies that his desire to work in the prison system has anything to do with finding who killed his wife, but again I can't help thinking that, deep down inside, the desire for revenge has never left him.

CHAPTER 14

Never to be released – or not?

ANITA'S KILLERS WERE ALL PETTY CRIMINALS, with records mostly dating from childhood that had escalated to rape and murder. It is at John's request that their lives are not dissected at length in this book. This account is not about them. It's about the destruction they caused to Anita, John, their families, friends and the many others who were affected in some way by her murder.

Here are Justice Maxwell's scant descriptions of them from his sentencing:

> John Travers was born on 27 February 1967 and was a single man. His criminal record began when caught in possession of Indian hemp and implements in 1980.
>
> The prisoner Murdoch is nineteen, having been born on 1 September 1967, and is a single man. He is said to be an associate of the criminal class. He has a short criminal history.
>
> The prisoner Leslie Murphy is twenty-four, having been born

on 6 February 1963, and is a single man. He is said to be an associate of the criminal class. He also has a criminal history and two of the offences were sexual assaults, in 1983, for which he received three years' penal servitude on each count, to be served concurrently.

The prisoner Michael Murphy is thirty-four, having been born on 31 October 1952. He is single and is also said to be an associate of the criminal class. He has a more serious criminal record and at the time of these offences was an escapee and was serving a sentence of twenty-five years and is due for release by way of remission in January 1993.

The prisoner Gary Murphy is twenty-nine, having been born on 5 September 1957. He is single and said to be an associate of the criminal class. He has a long criminal record consisting mainly of stealing and breaking and entering. He also has a recognizance at the time of the commission of these offences.

On that historic day when they were sentenced, the five were given no hope of ever being released from jail. Justice Maxwell set no parole dates and stated plainly that their sentences were to be for life.

But while researching this book, I learned a sickening fact: these men do have a glimmer of hope of applying for parole. Nine years after Justice Maxwell handed down his sentence in Darlo Court, a quiet piece of legislation appears to have brought undone his stringent decree that these killers should never be released.

A Correctional Services background briefing note on the file of the killers makes it quite clear that Justice Maxwell's sentence was not ironclad:

'These five offenders were all sentenced to life imprisonment with a recommendation from the court they never be released. Under the *Crimes (Sentencing Procedure) Act* 1999, these offenders will be eligible to apply to the Supreme Court of NSW for the determination of a non-parole period for their sentence.'

The likelihood is slim, and John Cobby, Anita's family and the detectives who worked on the case will do everything in their power to make sure it doesn't even come close to a reality. But the legal possibility exists.

The note continues: 'As they are the subject of non-release recommendations, they are only eligible to make this application after serving thirty years of their sentence. The offenders may only make one application to the Supreme Court. If the Supreme Court declines to set a non-parole period, the offenders will be required to serve their existing life sentences.'

All five were sentenced in June of 1987, but the legislation is effective from the time when they were arrested for the murder of Anita – meaning that as of 24 February 2016, John Travers can apply to the Supreme Court for parole. Within weeks of that date, his fellow killers will also have the same right.

The note goes on: 'As the offenders are the subject of non-release recommendations, they are not eligible for a determination unless the Supreme Court is satisfied that special reasons exist that justify making that application.'

It appears the only special reason that could have any validity is if the applicant can prove that he is dying.

Some lawyers believe there may be other grounds, however. Leading Sydney criminal lawyer Simon Joyner, of Matouk Joyner Lawyers, has researched the legislation and analysed the legalities relating to the five convicted killers. Could they somehow find a loophole in order to gain release from jail?

Mr Joyner says there are two separate legal definitions that apply in this situation: 'life imprisonment' and 'imprisonment for their natural life'.

'An example of the first one is where somebody is sentenced to life imprisonment but has a non-parole period of thirty years. There is still a possibility they will get out of prison. However, where somebody is in prison for their natural life, they are in prison until they die,' he advises.

This is crucial for the men convicted of Anita Cobby's murder. 'They are serving life imprisonment without a non-parole period set, while saying "never to be released", they were not sentenced to prison for their natural life.'

According to Mr Joyner's research, on 7 December 2006, there were indications that Gary and Leslie Murphy intended to apply for a release date, but Joyner found no evidence that any applications were made to the Supreme Court on their behalf, or on behalf of any of the offenders convicted of the murder.

As to the question of whether they are eligible to apply for parole, despite the sentence they received, Joyner informs me that it is out of the question. Simply put, they cannot go to the State Parole Authority after thirty years and ask to have their parole looked at. The authority can only consider releasing an inmate on parole when they have served the non-parole period, but Justice Maxwell deliberately declined to set a non-parole period, meaning they should never be eligible for release.

There is, nevertheless, a possible loophole. 'They can apply to the Supreme Court to have their sentence re-determined under clause 2, schedule 1 of the *Crimes (Sentencing Procedure) Act 1999* (NSW). This is an application where the applicant asks the court to reconsider setting a non-parole period so the inmate might become eligible for parole. The court cannot reconsider the overall head sentence in this case because of the non-release recommendation. These men will never be released unless a parole order is granted.'

There are strict criteria that must be satisfied before the

court will make an order setting a non-parole period for an inmate the court has recommended should never be released:

1. They must have served thirty years of their sentence before applying.
   a. They were taken into custody in late February 1986. Assuming their sentences began from that time, they can apply for re-determination in late February 2016.
2. They are not eligible for a re-determination unless the Supreme Court is satisfied that 'special reasons' exist.

According to Simon Joyner, one case similar to that which could apply to the Cobby killers has already been before the courts. Alan Baker and an accomplice, Kevin Crump, were sentenced to life imprisonment plus fifty-five years back in 1973 for the murder of a New South Wales housewife, Virginia Morse. It bears similarities to the murder of Anita Cobby: a random stranger was abducted and repeatedly raped before being tied to a tree and shot.

In 1997, the New South Wales Government passed legislation to make sure both Baker and Crump would stay in jail until they died – similar to Justice Maxwell's intention for the Cobby killers. Both Baker and Crump challenged the New South Wales law in separate cases in the High Court of Australia, but in October 2004 each lost. In other words, the High Court supported the New South Wales Parliament's sentencing laws with respect to life imprisonment.

Kevin Crump had his sentence set at a minimum of thirty years back in 1997 and has had three parole applications rejected. In May 2012, the High Court ruled that Crump had no grounds to appeal the law, finding he is to stay in jail until he is physically incapacitated or close to death.

In its decision against Baker, the High Court said a number of factors had to be considered before a prisoner could be granted leave to appeal for parole and the circumstances would have to be extraordinary for any judge to make such an order, as is the case with the Cobby killers. The fact that an offender seems to have been largely rehabilitated wasn't enough on its own.

The situation remains that the five have only one shot at making an application, and if that application is unsuccessful, then their sentences will be for the rest of their natural life.

They could mount an appeal against such a decision to the Court of Criminal Appeal, however, and if that application were to succeed and the court were then to make an order setting a non-parole period, they would be eligible for parole. Subsequently, they could make an application to the State Parole Authority (SPA) when the non-parole period expires.

Fortunately, the Parole Board itself has strict guidelines it must follow because of the non-release order. If, in the unlikely case the five Cobby killers are granted the right to seek parole, there are still a number of stumbling blocks they will have to overcome before they will have any chance of seeing the outside world.

The Parole Board has to have proof from the Chief Executive Officer of Justice Health that the offender:

- is in imminent danger of dying, or is incapacitated to the extent that he or she no longer has the physical ability to do harm to any person, AND
- has demonstrated that he or she does not pose a risk to the community, AND
- is further satisfied that, because of those circumstances, the making of such an order is justified.

Says Mr Joyner: 'In summary, [the Cobby killers] cannot apply for parole as their present position now stands but they could if they make a successful application to have their sentence re-determined and get a non-parole period set. If the court declines to set a non-parole period, they will be in prison for their natural life.'

Through hours of researching relevant cases and the *Crimes (Sentencing Procedure) Act* 1999, Mr Joyner believes there is a legal possibility the five men could try to get a non-parole period set. 'But their chances are less than slim in my opinion,' he says.

It takes a bit of adjusting to – the idea that there is even a remote possibility of parole for the so-called Cobby killers. Because of the serious nature of the offence and lengthy period of incarceration, a Parole Board would have to consider whether to grant parole – whether, for instance, having these individuals walking the streets might put the safety of the community at risk; whether those guys are sorry for what they did.

I know someone – a former colleague – who was curious about what it was like to be sentenced to life in jail and who several years ago had a lengthy chat with one of the killers. *Sunday Telegraph* reporter Julie Nance had previously published a series of articles about jail experiences for both male and female inmates. The Corrective Services authorities were impressed with her work, so when Nance was researching a story in 1994 on 'lifers', they offered her the opportunity to interview maximum-security prisoners, providing that Nance's questions focused strictly on the prisoners' experiences of life in jail, not their crimes. That's how she was given access to three of the state's worst killers.

Corrective Services chose the inmates – to be interviewed on the same day – three men who moved in a small circle of twenty-two 'at risk' prisoners. They were notorious inmates, isolated day and night from the mainstream Lithgow jail population of

263. The first was John Glover, known as the 'Granny Killer', who had murdered six elderly women in 1989 and 1990. The next prisoner was the 'Lonely Hearts' killer, Rodney Cameron, who met his victim through a Melbourne radio matchmaking program, ending her life only three months after being released from a 16-year jail term for two other murders. The last inmate interviewed by Nance was one of the Anita Cobby murderers, Michael Murphy. The eldest of the three Murphy brothers charged with that crime, at the time of the murder he was aged thirty-three. And he was a jail escapee.

When I quizzed Nance recently about her extraordinary encounters, she told me it was a disturbing assignment. 'I was very surprised Corrective Services chose such high-profile prisoners for me to interview,' Nance said. 'It was a nerve-racking experience, having each of these murderers being led one by one into a room to sit with me at a table, with the photographer and a guard standing far off in a corner.'

Both Glover and Cameron told Nance that given the multiple murders they had committed, they should never be freed. Cameron even said that capital punishment would have been fitting for his crime. However, Murphy told Nance he believed jail had made him a better person and he deserved to one day be free to rejoin society. At the time of the interview Murphy was undergoing Year 10 high school study and had been involved in other courses.

The following is an extract from the interview:

Once you give up on hope, you're history – you'd probably never recover from it. I have to be realistic about it. I know there is a chance I will never get out . . . but also a chance that I will. If I started thinking I had no chance, I might as well lie around and do nothing. At one time I just didn't care – I wouldn't do anything. But now, especially since I have been in this jail [Lithgow], I've changed my whole attitude.

I've taken part in woodwork – making trucks and jewellery boxes . . . I've done conflict resolution, an AIDS program, a course in sewing and now tailoring and menswear.

It would be stupidity to stick people in prison and take everything away from them. If you send someone who cannot read or write to jail and they don't do anything [to learn], you'd be sending them out the same way you sent them in.

People have the right to their own opinions, but who are they to determine if someone should ever get out of jail? They don't know what the person is really like. People do change.

Take me, for example. I've set myself on a program to better myself as much as I can. I've never really started on a goal and gone on with it [until now].

For eight and a half years I've been here [in jail protection] so to go out in the main part now, I'd be paranoid. The only difficulty is we are locked up earlier here, but they are going to change all that. When I go to my cell, I watch TV, depending what's on, but I mostly watch videos and they have two a night. My other interest is football.

I ring my family all the time – every week – and I was getting visits all the time, but I got sick of them. Letters are the same – you write one and might as well not write another for six months.

Mum and Dad are separated, and it's hard for them both – having four of us on the inside. I haven't seen Mum for about twelve months, and my father had a few heart attacks and has retired.

I've had enough of jail. When I was younger, jail meant nothing to me. As you get older, you realise what it is really like to be here and what you could be doing out there. I have lost a lot. My kids have grown up without me. I have two daughters, nineteen and seventeen. They have seen me a few times, but it's pretty hard for them.

On hearing those last few words, John Cobby almost explodes. 'It just makes me want to kill him, his brothers and the other two even more.'

Contemplating the slightest chance that any of these five animals will ever be released visibly disturbs John Cobby. It's a harrowing possibility as he tries to renew his life.

He and I endlessly debate the wisdom of including the legal discussion in this book and letting 'those scum' know of the existence of a potential legal avenue open to them. In all reality, they would be aware of it anyway. Michael and Gary Murphy have already attempted to challenge their sentences.

They may be uneducated but they have razor-sharp survival instincts. No doubt they are well informed too, having been exposed to thirty years of jailhouse lawyers, prisoners who spend their time inside frequenting the prison library. Many fancy themselves as smarter legal advocates than those operating outside.

Something John constantly says is 'I want the public to know and to help me stop [any release].'

John has never known all their names. He knows there are a 'couple of brothers' but that's the extent of his knowledge.

'I don't want to know about or hear about their horrible upbringing. There are no excuses.'

Former detective Graham Rosetta was also reluctant to talk about 'the five' for the book. He gave a number of reasons, one being that he didn't want Travers, Murdoch and the three Murphy brothers to get any recognition. 'They are indescribable human beings. The only kind of half-decent thing [Travers] ever did was pleading guilty. And that's not saying a lot.'

If Travers were ever to get out, Rosetta says he would worry about the safety of anyone who had had a hand in putting him away – and of the public at large. 'Travers's eyes were the coldest I have ever seen. Nothing he would do would shock me.'

The three Murphy brothers are currently together in the maximum security section of Goulburn jail, which bewilders John and the police involved. Why would they let these three be near each other?

Michael Murdoch was in a medium security jail until July 2015, when it became known that he and other lifers, such as Andrew Garforth, the killer of schoolgirl Ebony Simpson, had been reclassified out of maximum security. After a campaign by the Sydney *Daily Telegraph*, the Corrective Services Minister David Elliot ordered they be returned to their rightful place in maximum security.

John Travers, the ringleader, is also in Goulburn jail.

From all reports, the five are nondescript prisoners, totally institutionalised, with very little standing in the prison hierarchy – in fact, quite the opposite.

When they were sentenced, Garry Lynch quietly expressed the hope – which he wasn't proud of – that they would suffer at the hands of other prisoners. It seems his prayers were answered.

Six months after the trial finished, Michael Murphy was again back in Darlinghurst court, to be sentenced for escaping from jail before the murder.

Speed Kennedy was there to read the statement of facts and yet again was able to eyeball one of the men he detested so much.

'When Murphy came up from the cells, he stood at the defence table while his lawyer asked the judge if his client could stand during the sentencing hearing, due to a medical condition. I was curious and went down to the cells later and asked around about what was up with Murphy and why couldn't he sit down.'

A prison guard told him Murphy had been assaulted by other prisoners and would be in no condition to sit for a long time.

'They told me some prisoners had held him down, inserted a piece of plastic tubing up his anus and then threaded barbed wire into it. They then ripped off the tubing, leaving the barbed wire inside the guy's body.'

There's a hint of a smile as he retells the story. 'I told Anita's father what had happened to Murphy.'

John heard the story from a neighbour in the mid-1990s while he was working at Long Bay jail. 'Funnily enough I never heard it when I was at work. It was a neighbour who knew a guard and told me. I hoped it was true.'

But when I raise the possibility that the men Kennedy helped lock up for life have some hope of again roaming the streets, his eyes get a cold stare as he remarks, 'God help us if they do.'

CHAPTER 15

An epiphany

January–February 2015

JOHN FRANCIS IS TWITCHY. It's the time of the year when he feels most vulnerable. Whenever the anniversary of Anita's death approaches, the drive towards self-destruction, ever present, becomes stronger. But this is going to be the year that breaks him, angers him and drives him to tell his story.

As always, it is his ever-protective sister who warns him. A memorial ceremony for Anita Cobby is being planned by a former detective chief inspector, Gary Raymond, who worked on the murder investigation.

John is bewildered, confused and then angry. *What the fuck! Who is this guy and why are they doing this now after all these years?* Just like when Peg Lynch died, John can't understand why people are still obsessed with Anita Cobby.

My phone rings. John is on the other end in a distressed state.

'Do you know about this memorial for Anita? What's it about? Are you going? Are you guys covering it? Do you think you will go? Gaynor just told me,' he says.

'Yes, I know about it. And yes, we will probably send someone to it because even now anything to do with Anita Cobby is a story Sydney can't forget about,' I reply.

What had also struck me was that the story about the memorial had been broken by Jessica Oxford, a young reporter working for a Blacktown newspaper. Her father, Russell Oxford, is one of the state's longest-serving and most respected homicide detectives. Now working with the Robbery and Serious Crime Squad, he had arrested Roger Rogerson in early 2014 for allegedly killing a young drug dealer, Jamie Gao. In recent years I had spent a fair bit of time with Rogerson, who despite no longer being a police officer had an incredible knowledge of the New South Wales Police Force and was a great story-teller. I spent many hours over boozy lunches with the former detective as he described some of the characters he had encountered during his career. Like the tow-truck drivers, detectives and lawyers who were contacts, he was invaluable to my reporting of crime in the city.

But none of it meant anything to an agitated John Francis.

As he was talking to me, the journalist in me screamed that with the memorial coming up, I had a big story at my fingertips – about him. But the friend in me said it was his story to tell, not mine. Over the years, it had frequently crossed my mind that all of this would make a great book. Whenever I had mentioned it to John over the years, he was always black and white, quick to tell me that there was no way.

'I don't need to bring up all that shit,' he would reply. And the fact that someone else was bringing it up now was upsetting him.

'Why now, after all these years, is there a memorial? It's been twenty-nine fucken years,' he exclaimed, bewildered and angry. 'Who is this guy?' he asked, referring to Raymond. Garry and Peg had always been Anita's voice, and to John it seemed that now they were dead, random strangers were picking over her body.

It hadn't been like that, as I eventually discovered. Gary Raymond had worked as a junior detective on the Cobby case. When I spoke to him, Raymond said he had seen a demand to honour and celebrate Anita's life following the recent deaths of her parents Garry and Grace and had been planning to organise a memorial on the thirtieth anniversary of Anita's death.

I talked to Raymond after the memorial took place on 2 February. He explained, 'I spoke to Anita's sister, Kathryn, about doing something to mark the passing of Anita after thirty years and Kathryn said, "Why not this year?" And it started from there.'

Raymond had gotten to know the Lynches fairly well. As a senior police officer at Blacktown, he would drop in on them from time to time to have a cup of tea. 'Garry always said to me he wanted something good to come out of Anita's death, for it not just to be remembered as a horrible crime. He didn't want her to be forgotten. Anita's murder traumatised the community at the time. It changed people's lifestyles. People no longer felt safe walking alone, and I remember people were buying weapons and wouldn't let their female friends or relatives go out alone. It really was a turning point in the way Sydney started to behave.'

Gary Raymond said he had been peripheral to the case but, like everyone else who had worked on it, it had touched him deeply. He'd been a young detective sergeant given responsibility for information-gathering. 'The photos of her injuries – it's something the likes of which I'd never seen before and have never seen again. They were shocking,' he said. 'People were ringing up the station every day at the time, asking why we hadn't caught who murdered her. The community went into lockdown. Everyone was terrified, afraid they would be the next victim. Men went to workplaces to pick up their wives, girlfriends, daughters or sisters. Blacktown had never been so quiet on the streets.'

Raymond had formed a strong connection with Anita's family over the years. 'Garry always said to me, "I want the community to never forget Anita." We put out 200 chairs for the memorial and more than 300 people turned up. Garry and Grace would have been touched. We are now trying to raise funds to build Grace's House in memory of Grace Lynch, where victims of homicide – especially children – can get some solace and support.'

Anita's only sibling, Kathryn Szyszka, who has always kept a low profile, spoke publicly about her big sister before the memorial: 'It could have happened to anyone's daughter. She was just walking home, and happened to be at the wrong place at the wrong time. But people should be free to walk on the street without being abducted – there shouldn't be a wrong place.'

I didn't know any of that when I was speaking to John Francis in January. To me it made no sense that Gary Raymond – or anyone else – would put on a memorial for anything but noble reasons. In that moment, however, I didn't have the answers John was seeking.

Above all, he wanted to talk, so we arranged to meet for coffee at Bronte Beach the next day.

His demeanour had softened now that twenty-four hours had gone by, but he was still angry. 'I've lived with this shit most of my life. Who cares now? Why? Why?' he repeated. Normally well-spoken and articulate, when he speaks of things he sees as injustices or – like on this occasion – when he thinks someone is meddling in his business, his life, John will change his language dramatically.

Over several cups of coffee, I tried to explain to him that Anita's murder had touched a chord in anyone who had been remotely involved in the case back then, and still touched them today, even those who weren't alive at the time.

The next words that came out of his mouth floored me: he was thinking of going to the memorial himself. 'Just to smash this guy . . .' he said, only half joking.

But he had no idea who Raymond was and had no logical reason to hate him. Inevitably, as the anger subsided, he had second thoughts about going and then rejected the idea – all in the same breath.

The day of the memorial came around. He didn't attend. But that night, he got absolutely plastered. Angry texts from him started popping up on my phone, decrying the day's events.

His anger didn't stop him from having a look on Facebook, where several pages are dedicated to the memory of Anita. What he saw there stunned him. There were hundreds of comments from total strangers – many from a generation far removed from the murder. People who weren't even alive when the crime was committed had attended the memorial and posted moving tributes about John's wife. While this confused him, at the same time it moved him deeply that people were so affected by Anita's death.

While in a drunken state, on the Facebook site John posted a photo of himself and Anita together. He did it under his own name, John Francis. It was the first time he had done anything so publicly linking himself to Anita.

Admittedly, few visitors to the site would have made the connection that the John Francis who had posted that picture was in fact John Cobby, Anita's husband, but it was a massive step. Maybe subconsciously John was getting ready to let his secret out.

The following day, now sober and reflective, John was on the phone to me again. This time there was a calmness in his voice as he spoke about the amazing reaction to Anita's memorial and his drunken online activities. Astonishingly, working through his reactions to this event seemed to have uncorked something in John.

We met the next day. When I pulled up a chair opposite him, 'It's time' were the first words he said.

The memorial and the Facebook tributes had been a catalyst. Now, the lifelong strain of being John Cobby was pouring out of him. And there would be no stopping it.

'I think I want to talk, tell everything, and then run like the bejeezus.' But, he stressed, he didn't want a 'shitty, sensational newspaper story'. With a grin, he added, 'No offence.'

It took a while for it to sink in, but John was finally going to talk publicly. It made me think of how we had met, nearly thirty years ago. Back then, getting John to talk was like getting blood out of a stone.

May–June 1987

The trial was underway. My employers at the *Daily Mirror* were very keen to interview 'the husband'. By then John had changed his name by deed poll, had made overseas trips on two occasions – essentially, he had fled twice – and had gone to extreme lengths to hide the fact he was Anita's widower.

'It was a horrible time,' Gaynor tells me now. 'People whispered behind your back – and still do. Some of the family got death threats. John just had to hide away.'

In the days and weeks immediately following the murder, anyone who asked about Anita's husband was met with blank stares and shrugs from police and evasions from the Lynch family. The detectives on the case and the Cobby and Lynch families all knew John was in the darkest of spaces after his wife's death and did everything to protect him. Garry's willingness to front the media took the spotlight away from John, and the killers became the focus of much of the media's attention after their arrest. John had been able to fade into the background. But as the trial was drawing to an end, news organisations were vying with each other to get the definitive Cobby story, some sort of exclusive. Anything to feed the public's insatiable appetite for the case.

Back then, afternoon newspaper circulation was in decline. The *Mirror* was selling around 250,000 copies a day and its rival the Sydney *Sun* around 200,000. Competition between the two was fierce. The unvarnished truth is that Anita's story sold. Every time her face was on the front page of the paper, sales increased significantly. Editor of the *Daily Mirror* Roy Miller said it was a crime story almost unrivalled in Sydney history.

'She was a beautiful girl from the western suburbs and abducted from the streets. It was where our readers were and they were frightened and felt personally involved. It touched them all.'

Even though I was a young reporter, Miller had given me six weeks to come up with something that the others didn't have. The pressure was on, but I was just one of dozens of reporters all over the city trying to get the ultimate exclusive.

There was a fairly straightforward list of people I could talk to. The Lynches were talking to everyone but had formed a special bond with a young journalist, Julia Sheppard, from the opposition newspaper the *Sun*. She was the same age as Anita and similar in looks, and became genuinely immersed in their grief. Julia went on to write a moving account of the murder called *Someone Else's Daughter*, and remained close to the Lynches until their deaths.

Detectives on the case were giving interviews after the trial without favour. No one was going to get a special break on such a horrific murder. They played it straight down the middle.

The killers were from disjointed families. They had plenty of criminal friends and dubious relatives who would say anything for notoriety or money: not good for what I wanted. Others were simply too scared or ashamed to be associated with the monsters.

After I'd spent some time in the western suburbs fruitlessly trying to find something to write about, and rumours that the Murphys' father lived in Glebe had come to nothing, I had to admit I was getting nowhere.

The only one left on my list was the long-forgotten husband. He was a total mystery. No one knew what he did for a living, where he was or if he was even in the country. Any family members contacted stonewalled all inquiries. The cops intimated that he was overseas and was off limits. 'Not in a good way,' was how one detective described John to me, and would say nothing more. As far as they were concerned, he was a victim of one of the worst crimes in Australian history, and if he wanted to stay hidden, they were not going to help any journalist find him.

Still shaken after his interview on the day Anita's body was found, John had not taken the cops into his confidence when he had changed his name. For all intents and purposes, John Cobby, husband of Anita, no longer existed.

But the efforts of John Francis, nurse and messed-up young man, to try to shut out the world were about to pause dramatically.

One Saturday, about three weeks before the end of the trial, I took a phone call from my chief of staff, John Choueifate.

'I've found the husband. He has changed his name but I've found him. We have to go and knock him up [knock on his door] today,' he said.

Had I not had a massive hangover, I might have expressed more enthusiasm. The previous night had been a big drinking session with the detectives and other journalists after yet another day in court. In a somewhat perverse way, all those involved in the case had formed a special bond with each other. Even though the journalists were competitive and the cops guarded, we would get together almost weekly to drink and discuss how things were going with the case. For years afterwards, this continued with regular lunches. The group called itself the 4MT Club – from the initials of the three Murphys, Murdoch and Travers. Garry Lynch would occasionally come along too for the first few years.

Anyway, on that Saturday morning in 1987, my head was hurting. The last thing I wanted to do was turn up at the house of this guy who had been so carefully avoiding any media attention. But Choueifate was not about to take no for an answer. We had to go now, he told me. He would pick me up from my unit in Bondi in thirty minutes. At those words, there was a click and the line went dead. I struggled into the shower and hurriedly did my best to make myself presentable.

There was little conversation in the car as we made our way to the Rockdale address. Choueifate won't say how he came by it, even to this day. Maybe someone in the then Motor Transport Department or Department of Births, Deaths and Marriages had earned themselves some pocket money by searching through the records. Choueifate was my age but years ahead of me in many respects. He had contacts all over Sydney – in the political world, the underworld and government departments. Normally he was an understated character, but I could tell he was excited. Someone had come through for him with information about Cobby's new identity, and we were on the verge of getting a major exclusive.

Around ten o'clock, we walked up to a small brick house in Rockdale and knocked on the front door. A woman in her late forties answered. As we explained who we were, her face registered shock and then concern.

'How did you find him?' she asked.

Choueifate mumbled something incomprehensible but said we didn't intend to expose where John lived, just to talk to him about the court case. Basically, he pitched the proposed story as John's chance to put into words his feelings for Anita – and the killers.

The veiled threat of exposure was there. I'm not sure whether it registered. Mrs Cobby was polite, if a little shaken, and said she would tell John when he got home and pass on my number. Unbeknown to us, John wasn't actually living with his mother but had accommodation in the nurses' quarters of the hospital where he was working. Terri Cobby was in no hurry to set us straight, of course.

On the drive back to my place in the eastern suburbs, Choueifate and I rated our chances of getting a phone call from John as negligible. If anything, we speculated, our visit would prompt him once again to take flight. But Choueifate, being a true news hound, dropped me home, returned to the office and started making phone calls. A few hours later, he discovered that John was working at Garrawarra Hospital, south of Sydney. Convinced that John was likely to flee at the first opportunity, Choueifate drove straight down there.

Choueifate's memory of that afternoon is a little foggy now, but he tells me that when he arrived he located the nurses' quarters in a secluded spot, a short distance from the hospital. 'It was almost in the National Park . . . John was shocked I'd found him. I remember going into a kitchen and talking to him. We talked for a long, long time. All he seemed to want to know was how I had found him.'

The newsman found it tough getting John to talk. 'We kept standing there in the kitchen and I told him we were doing the story after the trial and it would be better if he helped us. It took a lot of convincing. I said he should ring Mark Morri, who would do the writing. I gave him the number and wondered if he would call. But I was confident.'

For his part, John has no memory of Choueifate's visit. Only that his world was unravelling because he had been found, and his anxiety was peaking. 'I would have drunk more than my usual bottle of scotch that night,' he remarks.

The following evening, at about 8.30, my phone rang. It was John Francis.

He had a soft voice, and he sounded scared. He asked me how we had found him and what we wanted. Summoning all my tact, I explained we wanted a chance to talk to him and let him tell his side of the story. Frankly, the cards were stacked in our favour: we knew where he lived and worked and his real name, and that if that information got out, all hell would break loose for him.

I don't remember in detail what I said, but it was not my proudest moment. This was the biggest crime story of my career and I couldn't let him go.

The conversation lasted a few minutes and arrangements were made to meet the following week. John did put his foot down about one thing: his sister was coming along. Gaynor had to be present or else it wouldn't happen, he said.

Choueifate, John, Gaynor and I met for dinner at one of Sydney's best restaurants south of the city – Le Sands, in Brighton le Sands – to talk things over. It was a beautiful restaurant and very discreet. We had booked a window table overlooking Botany Bay, and during lulls in conversation, we could watch the planes take off across the water from Mascot airport.

John was obviously nervous and suspicious of both of us. At one stage he looked at a plane ascending from the runway then glanced at me. 'I wish I was on that. This is terrifying.'

Much of the talk was about horses – anything to relax him. Both keen followers of the races, the two Johns swapped anecdotes and tips about the form of the current batch of racehorses. Gaynor and I made small talk and the four of us studiously avoided the elephant in the room.

What Choueifate and I really wanted was for John to spill his guts about his wife, who had been raped and murdered. It was hardly the stuff of good dinner conversation.

Not really knowing what to say, I drank quite a lot and had to make several trips to the bathroom. Years later, John and Gaynor told me they thought I was leaving the table to replace tapes in some secret recording device they imagined I had on me.

Eventually, John Choueifate took the bull by the horns and said we were keen to do a series of articles with John about his life with Anita and what had happened afterwards.

John didn't warm to the idea of going public. He was frightened and didn't want to be exposed to hordes of media – in fact he was panic-stricken. But Choueifate and I cajoled and made assurances that we wouldn't let anyone know who he was or where he was. It wasn't in our interests for other media to know his location or his real name. Hanging over the conversation was the menace that John's new identity would be revealed if he didn't co-operate.

John had the look of a man who knew he was cornered. A couple of times, he and Gaynor walked away from the table; they also asked Choueifate and me to leave them for a moment so they could talk privately.

Someone brought up the subject of money. Either Choueifate – to try to get John over the line – or John himself.

John remembers wanting an overseas trip. 'I was broke and wanted to run again,' he says. 'I don't think I'd been back in Australia long and you guys showing up on my doorstep when I thought I was safe from the media, it really rattled me.'

Negotiations went back and forth between John, Gaynor and Choueifate. Various possibilities were weighed up. It appeared that what John wanted was to go to the Gold Coast and spend time with some friends, so he would be away from Sydney when the story broke. Eventually it was agreed that the *Mirror* would pay for him and his sister to go wherever they wanted to go interstate and would keep his identity secret. In return John would tell his story, and hand over some photos of himself and Anita.

The way John saw it, he didn't have much choice. His identity had been uncovered and the *Mirror* would have written the story without him, staked out his mother's and sister's home to get a picture, or, worse still, let the TV stations know where they were.

It was settled, and we agreed to meet for several days in a row at the Marco Polo Motel in Randwick, a stone's throw from the racetrack where John had spent so much of his time.

Over three consecutive nights, John Choueifate and I sat in a motel room with an old cassette player, taping the interviews.

Everything went as planned, yet nothing about the process was easy. The strain on John was audible in his voice. He was hard to pick up on the recorder when we first tested it and we had to ask him repeatedly to speak up. Here was a man who had become introverted and suspicious of everyone. His confidence was non-existent. He spoke haltingly. Every now and again he would break down. But, bit by bit, he told us the story of his life with Anita.

When he got to the part where he found out about the murder, the tears started to cascade down his face and he asked for the tape to be turned off. He put up his hand up and said, 'Stop, please.' But when I went to push the pause button, Choueifate said, 'No. Let's get through this.'

His argument was that if we stopped all the time, it would be more drawn out for John and he would have to repeat the story and the heartache all over again.

'I didn't like him for that. Really didn't at all,' John says, shaking his head. 'You were okay, seemed a bit more understanding, but I still didn't trust you.' He tells me this years later, but at the time I knew full well how much pain he was in.

Those interviews drained him. It was obvious he was being

coerced into talking and it was not cathartic in any way. The process was painful for all concerned. Drawing information out of him was excruciating and not a pretty thing to be part of. Nevertheless, we pushed on and put together a series of three articles.

The first appeared in the *Daily Mirror* on Monday 15 June under the headline 'THE ANITA I LOVED'. As expected, sales soared by more than 20,000 a day.

John never read a word of the three-part series and still hasn't. As promised, by the time of publication, John and Gaynor were on the Gold Coast, keeping a low profile, and the *Daily Mirror* picked up the tab. John Choueifate was there too, as a kind of minder, to make sure no other media found him. The paper's editor, Rocky Miller, had told Choueifate, 'Go with them, enjoy yourself and make sure they are okay.'

Recalls Choueifate, 'We went to dinner a few times with John and some of his racing mates and went to the races as well.'

I hope some members of the group had a good time. It's doubtful whether John Francis did. He was like an automaton, walking and talking and appearing to function, but there was no life behind his eyes.

1987–2014

After the series ran, every now and again I would ring Gaynor to see how John was going, and occasionally I spoke to John himself. Something inside was telling me I couldn't just get this guy to spill all his emotions then walk away; it didn't seem right.

A few months later, Gaynor mentioned a party she and John were going to in Forest Road, Bexley. She invited me to come along and I accepted. There wasn't a story in it for me, but I liked John and Gaynor and thought, *Why not go and catch up with them?*

It was a cold night and I was wearing a long trench coat, perhaps getting a little carried away with being an up-and-coming crime reporter.

When we talk now, John remembers how Gaynor dragged him along to the party – still trying to get him out of his reclusiveness. And the sight of me in my trench coat stuck in his mind too. It brings a smile to his face. 'After you left the party, Gaynor and I reckoned you'd had some secret tape recorder in your jacket and we laughed about it. We liked you but still didn't trust you.'

By then the Cobby case was essentially finished. And after that first year of seeing John occasionally, I lost contact with him.

A couple of years went by, then the *Daily Mirror* got wind of a story that Gary Murphy had been bashed in jail. I was asked to find John again and get his reaction for an article.

Somehow I tracked him down at Gladesville Hospital, where he was again working the graveyard shift, dealing with ageing psychiatric patients after his switch to psychiatric nursing. He says he made the career change because he knew what it was like to be a 'broken' person. He felt sympathy for those who had tormented minds, but was also motivated by the need to try to understand himself. 'Now when I look back I think I was hoping that I could find a miracle cure for myself.'

One night at about eleven o'clock, I drove out there in an attempt to get a comment from him about Murphy's bashing.

John came to the back door of the hospital, looking nervous and drawn. It was an uncomfortable meeting. I explained to him that one of Anita's killers had been bashed and that he might want to say something. Such a look of pain came over his face that I felt sick to my stomach about being there. John had no desire to see his old name in print again. I promised him I wouldn't mention his old surname again as we had in the series of articles.

He told me that after the stories in the *Daily Mirror* some staff at the hospital where he worked had recognised him, even though the photo was old, and physically he had changed dramatically. Being recognised had shaken him badly.

Our conversation lasted only a few minutes. John had to get back to work. But before he closed the door, he said words to the effect that if I really had to, I could make up some line but, really, he wanted nothing to do with any news story.

I went back to the office and left a message saying that I believed John was overseas again. From the look of him and the way he spoke, it was evident that he was still going through an enormous amount of pain. It just wasn't worth adding to his torment for one line in a story.

A number of times over the following years, one of the Cobby killers would hit the news. In 1996, for instance, John Travers tried to escape while being transferred from Goulburn jail to Sydney for medical reasons. On occasions like those, I didn't bother to look for John Francis. I always told the bosses I had no idea where he was. It was obvious to me that he had already had enough media attention to last him a lifetime. Where some individuals I've dealt with would have welcomed an opportunity to voice their opinions, John simply acted like he was being hounded, and I didn't want to be the one inflicting that on him anymore.

So it came as a huge surprise when, one Sunday morning in the office around 2000 or 2001, a colleague rang and said a John Francis was on the line; did I want to take the call? The name registered immediately.

Out of the blue, John was on the other end of the phone, asking if I wanted to catch up. He didn't say why. It had been years since we had spoken and I wondered what he wanted. We agreed to catch up at Maroubra later in the week and I hung up, intrigued.

On the appointed morning, the rain was hosing down and the wind was howling. As we sat across from each other at a beachfront café near the surf club, I was disappointed to discover that John had no idea why he'd wanted to see me.

'I don't know why I called,' he said. 'I was working at Long Bay, and there were some pretty interesting characters there. I thought maybe if I found a story there or heard something you might be interested in, I might get another holiday out of you,' he said jokingly.

For the next hour we caught up on each other's news. John told me he had two kids and spoke about them with pride. That was something I could relate to, as I had just become a father as well. Anita never came up in the conversation. At the end of it, we exchanged numbers and each went off on our merry way.

I don't think we spoke much for the next couple of years, until one day I was traversing the coastal walk from Bondi where I lived to Bronte Beach – and noticed a heavily tattooed guy standing on the sand with a board under his arm. It looked a lot like John Francis but I kept walking. Curiosity got the better of me so I rang the number in my phone for John.

'It's Mark from the *Tele*,' I said. 'Were you on Bronte Beach yesterday, tattoos down one side, carrying a surfboard?' To be honest, I was feeling a bit like an idiot as I spoke.

'Yep, I live here now. Surprised you recognised me. We'll have to catch up for a beer or coffee.'

Over the next ten years, we would bump into each other regularly at the beach and chat about the football or the weather. It turned out John had moved into the area after he and his wife had broken up, and he was living a pretty solitary life. Whenever we chatted, I'd walk away thinking that John's secret and his life were an incredible story. Occasionally we would talk about Anita, and I'd say if he ever wanted to write a book, I'd be happy to do it.

His response never varied: 'Don't think so. I really couldn't face it all now. I'm safe in my Bronte bubble, as I like to call it.' A phrase he repeated many times over the years was 'I live under a rock and like it that way.'

Now someone had kicked his rock.

CHAPTER 16

Starting on the book

February–March 2015

IN THE DAYS FOLLOWING THE MEMORIAL, John and I spent hours discussing how we would do the book and what the consequences would be, not just for him but also for his family. Over and over he asked why I thought anyone would care about his life with Anita and what had happened to him since. As best I could, I assured him it was a powerful story – and I didn't even know the half of it, just bits and pieces from three decades ago, and what I'd picked up through the odd conversation with John on the beach over the last few years. To me, his story and his insights into Anita were compelling. I was sure people would want to read about them.

For a short while, we thought about having him do the book as 'John X', not revealing his new name, and not including any recent photos. That way he could continue to be the anonymous husband of the last thirty years. But something held John back. 'That's being a coward again, like I always have been. Maybe it's time to let people know what these animals have done to me, everyone around me and a whole bunch of people I don't even know.'

The waves were pounding Bronte Beach, and I suspected John was longing to be out there, back in his bubble, alone with the surf and total anonymity. Yet something was stirring in him. 'Maybe it's time,' he mused again, more to himself than to me, and gazed out to the waves.

Only a handful of people knew about John's past. How would his two children, ex-wife and sister react to his going public? He also had to weigh up the potential impact once everyone at his workplace and where he lived found out.

Similar thoughts had occurred to me. I told John there was no way I would write the book if his family didn't agree. 'I wouldn't fucken let you,' he said.

The next day, he announced that he had spoken to his sister and children and they were all for it, especially Daniel, his son. Even though Daniel hadn't ever known Anita, he had felt the impact; his father's trauma had had a big effect on him. So had keeping the secret as a teenage boy.

John was stunned by how supportive all his family were. 'I honestly thought they would tell me not to be stupid, and say, "As if anyone would care." Daniel, my son, said he was over the moon, and my daughter, Aerin, said to do it if I want . . . They said it's about bloody time.'

There was one last person John wanted to speak to before we got under way. That was Anita's sister, Kathryn Szyszka. If we went ahead with the book, he wanted to give Kathryn a chance to have input, and thought she would also have a better memory about things back then, considering his state of mind at the time.

Gaynor had remained in contact and was able to give me Kathryn's email address. In fact, she had already let Kathryn know John was thinking of doing a book. I sent Kathryn an email, asking if she would let me come and visit her to talk about her sister.

It was two weeks before Kathryn replied to me:

Hi Mark.

Sorry for the delay in responding. I just needed some time to digest and think things over.

I am pleased that John seems to be coming out of the shadows and taking this step in wanting to share his story (although I have not yet spoken to him). However I do not feel that I am in the position to provide much more than my support. I feel that things have been covered. It is now almost 30 years after the event. I found that my involvement in the recent memorial to mark the 29th anniversary of Anita's death took quite a lot out of me. At this stage in my life I'm trying to do my best to be a wife and mother, raising my two teenage children and providing them with a happy and stable environment. Every time Anita's story is brought up, it inevitably affects both my husband and my children.

I would hope for John's part that this might be cathartic for him, to finally deal with things and address his feelings.

Perhaps we could set up a meeting between yourself, John and me to discuss things further.

Regards,

Kathryn

John was reluctant to meet Kathryn, not only because of how emotional it would be for him but also because he could see from the tone of Kathryn's email that it would be incredibly painful for her as well. He told me to leave her alone.

'She was so close to Anita and they grew up together. She lost a sister who she obviously loved so much. She knew Anita a lot longer than me, and is such a nice person.'

To John, his sister-in-law was as big a victim of Anita's murder as he and her parents. She too had been scarred for life and was finding her own way to deal with it. He had no intention of adding to her pain if she didn't want to be involved.

Quietly, I was starting to freak out myself. John's timing left a bit to be desired, because by then it was only a week before my wedding. As I was preparing for one of the happiest days of my life, John had decided to talk about the saddest time of his.

Late February 2015

The first interview takes place in John's flat. It's small and cramped, and you can hear the waves pounding on Bronte Beach, only 200 metres away. He is sitting near a window, a glass of red wine in his hand. When he first starts to speak, his voice is shaky and I'm sure it isn't his first drink today, even though it's only about five o'clock. He hands me a beer, Crown Lager, which he has bought especially for me.

'I'm scared. I don't know if this is the right thing. Does anyone care?' he repeats.

Now, with a recorder in front of him, and the reality that his secret world will soon become public property, he is getting cold feet.

Images spring to my mind of the motel room in Randwick in 1987. We were doing almost exactly the same thing then, and it was awful.

But this time it is different. John wants to do it. He and I have become friends.

When I stop and think about it, we have spent the last couple of decades talking about his emotions.

I can do this, I tell myself, surprised to realise that my shoulders have become a little tense.

John Francis takes a gulp of red wine, draws in a deep breath and looks at me. 'Be gentle. I think this is going to hurt, but I think I gotta do it.'

I believe him, though his attempt to be resolute is not all that convincing.

For the next few hours he pours out his life story, crying at times. When he recounts a happy memory, a smile crosses his face. An ugly shadow plays across his features when anything comes up about the killers and what he would like to do to them.

Darkness falls and I go home to my wife. I feel uneasy as I leave John alone in his flat, with his bottles of red and a kind of fug of emotion in the ether from the truckload of memories he has just relived.

The next night, it's more of the same. Red wine, tears and smiles, sometimes savage mood swings. At times we go through the same things over and over again. Red-rimmed eyes meet mine. 'I want to kill them . . . kill them every way imaginable,' he says. I keep breathing and we press on.

We clock up five days of interviews and have two days off. More than once in that first week he decides it is a stupid idea, this book, and urges me to forget about the whole thing.

Before the second week gets under way, he texts me and says he is going to Coffs Harbour because he has to get away, that although he has lived with the memories every day, it is another thing altogether to talk about them openly like this.

Gaynor has warned me that John will try to run away. But she desperately wants him to stick with it, as does his son Daniel.

When he comes back from Coffs Harbour a few days later, John seems a little calmer. We continue with the process, but go over much of the same stuff all over again. This time, however, details emerge that he didn't mention thirty years ago, or even the previous week. It dawns on me that he has made a pact with himself, and when he suggests drawing up a contract between us – 'To protect you, in case I want to run away again, and I do every day' – I am confident I don't need it. I can't see John running out on me now.

For the next few weeks, we meet nearly every night and drink and talk. A barely perceptible change comes over him. Or so it seems.

Gaynor confirms my impression, assuring me the process is helping John, as well as her family. 'Honestly, he seems more relaxed than he has been in years. It's helping him come to terms with something he has kept locked up inside for thirty years.'

Slowly, slowly, it continues. Now, even when he fantasises about killing his wife's murderers, although the hatred is still evident, the ugly face has dissipated. Even some of the lines in his face seemed to have vanished. He is becoming more and more relaxed in talking about Anita, and our relationship is shifting.

'You are an important part of this, you know. I couldn't talk to anyone else about this. You never gave me up for thirty years. I trust you, and I haven't trusted anyone new in my life for a long, long time. *And* you're a journalist,' he adds, rolling his eyes with a smile.

When I sit down to interview Gaynor for the book, she describes how relieved she was when John rang her in January to tell her he had contacted me and was thinking about letting his secret out.

'*Thank God* was my first thought,' says Gaynor. '"About bloody time," I told him. We have lived with this for thirty years. It was like a dirty little secret that no one could talk about for John's sake.'

When she told John about the upcoming memorial, she was

heartened to see that for the first time he was expressing anger instead of fear about seeing Anita's name in the news. 'That was the first time I saw a shift in his emotions . . . I didn't realise how big a leap he had made but I'm glad he did.'

Gaynor felt she would benefit from finally telling her part of the story as well – her grief at losing not only a sister-in-law and very dear friend, but a brother along the way. 'To see him go from what he was back then to what he became after Anita's death was devastating to all of us.'

John's family noticed an immediate change in him when he met Anita, and Gaynor saw how her own relationship with John changed for the better as well. 'We were a small family. John and I were each other's only siblings and we became very close.

'John is four and half years older than me. As children we had a love–hate relationship. But as we got older, he became my protector. I was in awe of him and all his good-looking friends. From his early teenage days, girls would come and go in John's life because he was so handsome and full of charm and charisma.

'None of the girls stayed for long. As his little sister, I always knew I was first in his heart. Things changed when he met Anita. He told me all about her and I knew this was different, that she was the one and she was staying for the long haul.'

Gaynor pauses. 'My world shrank a little and I felt jealous of this girl I didn't even know, as I thought she would take John away. That was until I met her. Little did I know I would sort of fall in love with her myself. It was hard not to. People seemed to fall under her spell. Her open heart encompassed all.'

From the moment John met Anita, the womanising stopped. 'To be honest, women used to throw themselves at him, but when he met Anita, he only had eyes for her. Really, it was a love story. That's what I want people to know: just how much in love they were, and what a beautiful person on the inside Anita was.'

They were also a physically striking couple, John with his suntanned skin and blond hair complementing Anita's dark looks.

'Picture-perfect,' comments Gaynor. 'Often, when John was at work, Anita – I called her Neat – would pop up the street to our tiny house with a freshly baked banana cake, saying she couldn't stay long and was just dropping off the cake. She wouldn't have any because she was on a diet. She had this perfect figure, but she was always on a diet. But then she would sit for hours and talk to my grandparents. Four or so hours would go by, then she would smile, look at the empty plate – we had polished off the cake – and then she'd go.'

Because John's new wife and his sister were almost the exact same age, and because John frequently worked night shift, Anita ended up spending evenings out with Gaynor.

'I'd watch her getting ready. Her stunning, long, brown ringlets went all the way down her back. She'd spend hours trying to iron her beautiful hair straight, and I would look at her, desperately wanting to have curls like her.' Anita favoured light-coloured clothes and wore ballet flats long before they became fashionable. 'She looked gorgeous in whatever she wore,' says Gaynor.

'Anita loved the simple things in life – a laugh, a cuddle – and she had a huge capacity for love. Writing letters, reading books and listening to music. She loved animals and had a special soft spot for dogs.'

Watching her brother and Anita together would fill Gaynor with warmth. This was a couple obviously in love. 'I have great memories of John and Anita sailing around on their little yacht with their dogs, with the sun shining and life being so wonderful. I just loved watching them being together.'

Anita and Gaynor would chat about music and the life ahead for John and Anita. 'Even to this day, I cannot listen to the Simply Red song "Holding Back the Years" without crying. I see Anita every time the song is played. It was her song.'

When John and Anita took time out from their relationship, Gaynor certainly didn't see it as a forever thing. 'The weekend before she died, it was a hot weekend and all three of us were in the pool at our nan's place at Rockdale cooling down. They were a couple then and I know Anita went back and stayed with John at his house that night.'

Gaynor adds that Anita stayed with her in the week before she died. 'It was my birthday coming up, and we went to St Georges Leagues Club on the Tuesday night. It was "Girls' Night Out" at the club, and we were drinking and dancing. Just having a good time, as you do at that age.'

The pair didn't talk much about the marital problems Anita was having with Gaynor's brother. 'But we were sitting at a table when a guy came up and asked Anita to dance.' Gaynor had seen that sort of thing happen a lot when the two went out on the town. 'When you saw how gorgeous she was, it was obvious men were attracted to her. Anita was polite and just said to the bloke, "No thanks, I'm married." She fully intended to get back with John and still considered herself married in that week before she died.'

She says of her brother in those days, 'John Cobby was so handsome. To me, he was male model material. He was funny, irreverent, kind, fun-loving, teasing, tormenting – crazy in some ways – and life was never dull or boring in his company, with his beautiful trusting and caring nature.

'I mourned the death of my beautiful brother John Cobby. He was replaced with an imposter known as John Francis, who I still love – but he is untrusting, cynical, mental, intolerant, bitter and doesn't like many people.'

For years, Gaynor felt shackled, a silent victim of Anita's death, living with the anxiety of expecting at any time to hear her brother had killed himself.

'It was constantly there, this thought one day he would be dead from suicide. I spent hours sitting with John, talking him out of suicide or his crazy ideas about robbing a bank or something stupid so he could be jailed and kill the murderers.'

Gaynor will never talk about it as a burden, but losing Anita put her in the public spotlight too, in her community and social circles. It had an impact on her future life, and though she bore the pressure without complaint, it bubbled inside and occasionally would rise to the surface.

'I'd had enough of it a couple of years after her death. One day, I put a photo of John and Anita on their yacht on the mantelpiece. I loved that photo. It summed up my memory of them together – windswept, with hair blowing everywhere and nothing else on their minds. I put it in a frame and put it out there.

'John came into the loungeroom and went off his head. I was sick of it and yelled at him, "We loved her too."'

It was one of the rare times when she permitted herself an outpouring of anger towards John about his inability to deal with Anita's death, and it stays with her today. The photo was taken down.

'To protect John for all those years, we didn't talk about Anita as normal families did. We hid our grief from him. It was a terrible dark secret that we kept to ourselves to help keep him away from everything, hide who he was and try and stay out of the spotlight. It was like walking on eggshells.

'Anita's beautiful photo now has pride of place in my bookcase, and I often find myself saying "hello beautiful" as I walk past.'

Later, when Gaynor married and became a mother, the burden of being a Cobby, the sister-in-law of the late Anita, hung over her. With John having changed his name, her father dead and no other male siblings to carry on the Cobby name, she kept it after her marriage. When her son Christian was born in 2003, her husband Peter took the incredibly selfless step of letting his son take the Cobby name.

'We kept Anita a secret from Christian for years as he was a soft, sensitive little boy. We decided to tell him about his beautiful aunty just before he went into Year 7. We felt he should know the truth from us rather than strangers.' Gaynor still lives in the area where she grew up, and many of the parents who had kids at Christian's school would no doubt know who Gaynor was and her association with Anita.

After telling Christian, his parents made him promise that if he had any questions to ask them and not go and search the internet.

'Now that we have told him about Anita, it feels like a huge weight has been lifted from us and we now talk openly about her. Now we can celebrate her life – rather than mourn her terrible death.'

CHAPTER 17

The end of the line

FOR MONTHS AFTER THE INTERVIEWS, John and I would meet at a Bronte café, where we would talk about the book and how things were going. I told him I had been given total access to the police running sheets of the investigation, which contained enormous amounts of information.

He didn't want to know the details of how Anita died but was happy when I told him that much of the detail he had given me about what he experienced was corroborated by the police files.

The truth was that I kept a lot of details secret from him, including the entry in the police file about her seeing another nurse after she and John had split. It was only a few lines long, but it disturbed me greatly.

One day, as I was leaving police headquarters at Parramatta, I bumped into the head of the New South Wales Homicide Squad, Detective Superintendent Mick Willing. We chatted, and he subsequently allowed me access to the files.

Ironically, they had been sitting in his office, having been dragged out of the archives by Detective Russell Oxford for a tribute to the detectives in October 2015. The officers who worked on the Anita Cobby case were given special recognition at a gala night attended by 2000 former and serving detectives. 'Every homicide detective, no matter how young they are, knows about the Cobby case,' Detective Willing told me as we chatted. 'All murders are horrible, but Anita's murder, the reaction and the work police did was exceptional.'

When I walked into his office, they were sitting there – two boxes of statements, some now barely legible. I spent hours over a number of days poring through the statements and running sheets in those two cardboard boxes.

When I ran into Detective Willing, he asked me how it was all going. I told him the files were giving me invaluable information and great insight into the investigation, but that maybe I was getting to know too much. He raised his eyebrows and gave me an inquiring look, as if prompting me to expand on what I had found out. So I stopped beating around the bush and explained what I had uncovered about how Anita had possibly been seeing someone after she and John had split. I said I didn't know whether John knew or whether I should mention it to him.

Detective Willing looked at me with a sympathetic face. 'A murder inquiry has no secrets, mate. It strips people of their privacy.'

That phrase would haunt me. Willing was right, I realised. Murder has no secrets. I was learning that fast.

Should I share the information with John? Maybe it was malicious gossip. There was no corroboration, no follow-up interview. What would be the point of putting John through the pain of having Anita's memory tarnished for something I couldn't verify?

Hours later that night, I went round to John's flat to go over some details about his early life with Anita. Again, I didn't mention the possibility that Anita had been in another relationship. By then I was totally convinced it had no relevance to the book.

16 May 2015

It is a Saturday morning like so many others. John and I are sitting drinking coffee in a café in Bronte. As we have on so many other occasions, we talk about the book and Anita. John is relaxed. Since being interviewed for the book, he tells me, his drinking has halved. It's so clear to me that he has become more relaxed. Even so, when he drinks there are still flashes of self-hatred. The self-loathing is never far from the surface.

The conversation returns to the break-up. I don't have a recorder or even a notebook on hand when he blurts it out. We are simply two friends having a chat. 'Yes,' he says, 'she was restless when we came back, but maybe there was another bloke. I've never mentioned it and we never spoke about it.'

But Gaynor rejects the idea that another person was involved in the couple's break-up: 'In my heart of hearts I know there was no-one else in either of their lives.'

Either way, John is unfazed. He has not the slightest doubt that at the time Anita was murdered, she and John were well and truly on the path to reconciling. There had been no screaming matches as the pair decided to take a break, just a sadness and an acknowledgement that they needed time apart. And they were coming to the end of that break. They had planned to go flat-hunting in the second week of February, they spoke on the phone constantly – and, of course, he had spoken to Anita on the day she died. It had been, he said, 'a pretty nondescript phone call about nothing in particular': the typical conversation of people who ring each other all the time and let each other know their day-to-day activities and thoughts.

'It shits me that people think we broke up because of my punting or that they told police Anita didn't want to get back together. They are talking without knowing the facts – things that only the two of us knew.'

Garry Lynch was quoted in Julia Sheppard's book *Someone Else's Daughter* as saying that Anita was coming to terms with not being with John. 'She said to me that she loved John with all of her heart and she would love him all her life, but she knew they wouldn't be together again.'

When John hears what Garry was telling people about their separation after Anita died, a dark look comes over his face. What immediately comes to my mind is the tricky relationship between the two men, and how quickly it had come to a head when Anita first went missing. From what John has told me, I know he was angry that Garry had waited before informing the police and hadn't rung any hospitals. The two men had vented at each other that night; it was probably the last one-on-one exchange they ever had, and it hadn't been pleasant. But John chooses his next words carefully.

'Look, I don't want to slag off at him, because he was Anita's dad and obviously loved her, but after her death I imagine he would have been blaming me for what happened. Christ, it's only natural. *I* blamed me. A lot of people did. And I still do. But we were so going down the path of being together again and I don't think Garry would want to admit that. We never thought the separation was permanent. We kept talking and being part of each other's lives forever.'

The weekend before the murder they had slept together, just like old times.

But it would never again be like old times. The following Sunday, Anita caught the 8.48 from Central station to Blacktown.

John believes in God, and he looks forward to being reunited with his beloved Anita in the hereafter. Once in a while, he pours out his heart to her. 'There is a plaque in the chapel at

Sydney Hospital, where she worked. I used to go there sometimes and talk to her.'

Now the chapel is off limits to the general public and can only be visited with the permission of the administration.

On the day of Peg Lynch's funeral, when John visited Anita's grave site, he talked to her. 'I told her I loved her and would one day be with her. Which I truly believe.'

April 2015

Stephanie Scott was a beautiful young teacher from the small southwest New South Wales town of Leeton, who suddenly vanished on Easter Sunday, 5 April. She was twenty-six years of age, loved by the community where she lived and adored by the pupils she taught. It was just six days until her wedding to childhood sweetheart Aaron Leeson-Woolley.

When Stephanie failed to meet her fiancé for a dinner date and then failed to come home on the Sunday night, he reported her missing to local police. The next day the story hit the headlines.

'Young bride disappears before wedding' was the theme of the coverage, and pre-wedding nerves a popular theory as to why she had gone missing.

By Tuesday the family of Stephanie had posted on social media that she was missing and they wanted help to find her. They gave radio, TV and newspaper interviews, hoping the public exposure would help.

I interviewed her mother, Merrilyn, over the phone on the Tuesday morning, and while she spoke calmly about her missing daughter she had a nagging feeling of worry. Mrs Scott was adamant her daughter would not have run away from the wedding.

'I am convinced something has happened to her. She was such a reliable and valuable person to the community. Sometime between 12 and 1 pm on Easter Sunday something has happened. She would not just disappear.'

The last time she had withdrawn any money was on Saturday morning, when she drove the 60-odd kilometres to Griffith and bought cufflinks with her bankcard.

The story was gaining momentum and the *Daily Telegraph* sent young crime reporter Ashlee Mullany to Leeton, while I worked the phones, trying to find out more information from local police and Sydney detectives who had been asked to assist with the investigation.

Everyone was now starting to back away from the theory that Stephanie had had pre-wedding nerves – in fact the opposite. All her family said she had been looking forward to the wedding, and the day before had been shopping for jewellery (including the cufflinks) and other items in preparation for the occasion.

My mind couldn't avoid making the connection with Anita. Stephanie was twenty-six, beautiful and a person who gave more to others than herself. She had gone missing on a Sunday and been reported missing on a Monday; those details exactly matched the case of Anita.

That night, after a long day, I headed to John's flat to continue our sessions for the book. While I was sipping a beer and John a red wine, my phone rang. It was the office with questions about a timeline in the paper showing the last movements of Stephanie and her fiancé.

John was listening and I could see the look in his eyes shift from one of mild interest to one of fascination. He quizzed me the minute the call ended and I explained the story.

The red wine glass was drained in one gulp. He looked at me. There was no need to mention Anita.

'You think the fiancé did it, don't you?'

It had crossed my mind; as when Anita went missing, the one closest to the victim immediately becomes a suspect. But like John, Aaron Lesson-Woolley had no involvement whatsoever in her murder. It would only be a matter of days before another man was arrested; he is now awaiting trial.

Words began pouring out of John in a stream of consciousness; it was obvious the young woman's murder had struck a nerve.

'Everyone immediately suspects the boyfriend, the husband or the lover. I feel so much for that young guy, and even though I was cleared I still live with the moment I was accused by police and others thinking I did it. I still believe some people out there think I had something to do with Anita's murder.'

He then brings up another high-profile murder, again a woman snatched off the streets, raped and killed. 'When I heard of what happened to Jill Meagher my heart went out for her husband too.'

Jill Meagher was a 29-year-old woman walking home from a pub after drinks with work colleagues in the Melbourne inner-city suburb of Brunswick on a Friday night in September 2012. She never made it home.

Like Anita and Stephanie, her disappearance made national headlines after husband Tommy Meagher reported her missing. Six days later her body was found in Gisborne South, about 50 kilometres north of Melbourne. Her killer, Adrian Ernest Bayley, pleaded guilty to Meagher's rape and murder and was sentenced to life imprisonment.

'I really feel for both of these guys. To have someone you love go missing for days and to have suspicion hanging over your head while you are going through so much pain . . . it's . . .' he says without finishing his sentence.

Even though his rational mind tells him that in more than three-quarters of murders involving females the partner is responsible, he still can't shake the anger and shame he felt when the finger was pointed at him.

When John first decided to talk about Anita's death, he concentrated on the effects it had on his life and the lives of those around him – like his sister Gaynor and his two children, even the police and lawyers who were involved in the case.

He turns to me, with a look of pain. 'But how many more victims were there that no one ever hears about?'

CHAPTER 18

The day John Francis died

APRIL IS JOHN FRANCIS'S FAVOURITE TIME OF THE YEAR. The weather is mild and the water warm, and the gentle offshore winds bring decent-sized waves to Bronte Beach. The backpackers have left Sydney, heading north for the warmer weather of Byron Bay on their way to Queensland. Bronte is quieter now, the way John likes it.

For the past two months he has dissected his life, from the time he was born to meeting Anita and the effect her death has had on him and his family.

The notion of killing himself is a constant, but somehow a saviour always appears to bring him back from the brink. Despite spending hours contemplating it and years of abusing himself to the point where he hoped he would just drop dead, he never did.

The sun was shining when John woke up at six o'clock on the morning of 16 April. *Not a bad day to kill someone*, he thought, with an ironic smile.

He grabbed his board and went for a surf. He was feeling relaxed about what he was going to do.

At midday, his son Dan knocked on the door. John was ready. He locked his flat and the pair drove to Bondi Junction, where they parked the car then caught a train to Central station.

First things first. Father and son walked down to Chinatown, then made their way to the Golden Harbour restaurant. They had been coming there regularly for yum cha since Dan was a toddler.

John drank a few beers as they talked about Dan's upcoming overseas trip, caddying for Jake Higginbottom. Neither broached the subject of what they were about to do that day.

Minutes later, the pair stood outside the building housing the New South Wales Registry of Births, Deaths and Marriages. John hesitated, took a deep breath, then looked at his son and said, 'Right, let's do it.'

What took place next was a dry, bureaucratic procedure. They filled out some paperwork and then were told their new names would be official in a few weeks. Certificates would be mailed to them.

For John it was an anticlimax. Dan's reaction was altogether different. He took his dad back home then went out and celebrated with friends. Later he talked to me about it: 'It was this huge relief. It was something I had been wanting to do for years. Dad was pretty quiet.'

The night before, Dan had posted this on Facebook:

Most of you know me as Dan Francis. I wanted to let you know that tomorrow, my father and I are changing our surnames back to Cobby (our original family name.) Nothing can change what happened to Anita almost thirty years ago but tomorrow we are taking a big step in the right direction to having a life with a touch of relief. This is a huge step individually and as a family. I couldn't be prouder of my dad and what he's achieved. Tough times don't last but tough people do.

As for John, he went into a sort of trance. It had been crystal-clear to him that John Francis had to go. He couldn't live any longer with the lie; John Francis wasn't who he really was. He had been thinking about it for a long time.

But could it be that simple? Was John Francis really dead, and was he now reborn as John Cobby? He opened a bottle of wine and stared out the window, and his thoughts turned to Anita.

It was hardly surprising that John's old identity didn't come back to him easily. Two days after his trip to the city with Dan, he and I were sitting in our regular café in Bronte, talking about how he felt about the name change, when two friends of mine happened to walk in.

Before I could properly introduce him, John glanced at me, put out his hand and said, 'John Francis. Pleased to meet you.'

The name hung in the air between us.

'It's not as easy as I thought it would be,' he said to me after they had gone. 'I've been John Francis longer than I was John Cobby.'

The following week, he changed his name on Facebook without fanfare or comment.

Another two weeks went by. Then he went in and told his supervisor at the Prince of Wales Hospital the whole story. She was astounded.

'She looked at me and said she remembered the murder but had no idea who I was. I don't know why I chose that day to tell her but I did. Just an impulse, I suppose.'

But everyone close to him was noticing that John was changing – relaxing and smiling more. There were still dark moods and weekends lost to depression, but they were less frequent.

Then in June, Fox TV screened an hour-long program about the murder of Anita Cobby and I mentioned it to John beforehand – more as a warning than anything else.

He called a couple of days later.

'I watched it. I recorded it and went to delete it time and time again, but then just said "Fuck it" and sat through it.'

I was speechless.

He broke the silence. 'It was bad. There were things I had no idea about . . .'

It was a turning point, however. After decades of steadfastly trying to avoid the details, he was now facing up to what had happened. He asked questions about the killers, about detectives in the case, although he didn't go into the detail of what had happened to Anita, which was touched on in the show.

Our work on the book was nearly over, and John went on a long holiday to Indonesia to get lost in the waves. Not long after he got back, I rang him to see how he was.

'Hello, John Cobby speaking.'

About the Author

Born in October 1961, Mark Morri grew up on Sydney's Lower North Shore, attending St Leo's College before joining News Limited as a copyboy in 1980 after finishing his HSC.

As a crime reporter in the '80s, he worked at the *Daily Mirror*, covering the Sydney gangland murders, the Father's Day bikie massacre and the abduction of Sydney schoolgirl Samantha Knight.

Promoted to Chief of Staff, he continued to specialise in crime reporting, covering the Port Arthur massacre in 1996 and the backpacker murders by Ivan Milat. He worked for a brief time on the *New York Post* before coming back to the *Daily Telegraph*, again as Chief of Staff.

Over the past thirty-five years, Mark has covered nearly every major crime in Sydney, building contacts throughout the police force (and the criminal world). He is currently the crime editor of the Sydney *Daily Telegraph*.

Mark is married, has one child and lives in Sydney's Eastern Suburbs.